The Philosopher's Ring—Wagner as Thinker and Dramatist

Studies in German Literature, Linguistics, and Culture

The Philosopher's Ring—Wagner as Thinker and Dramatist

Michael Steinberg

Rochester, New York

Copyright © 2026 Michael Steinberg

All Rights Reserved. Except as permitted under current legislation, no part of this work may be photocopied, stored in a retrieval system, published, performed in public, adapted, broadcast, transmitted, recorded, or reproduced in any form or by any means, without the prior permission of the copyright owner.

First published 2026
by Camden House

Camden House is an imprint of Boydell & Brewer Inc.
and of Boydell & Brewer Limited
www.boydellandbrewer.com

Our Authorized Representative for product safety in the EU is Easy Access System Europe – Mustamäe tee 50, 10621 Tallinn, Estonia, *gpsr.requests@easproject.com*.

ISBN-13: 978-1-64014-245-9 (hardback)
ISBN-13: 978-1-64014-246-6 (paperback)

Library of Congress Cataloging-in-Publication Data
CIP data is available from the Library of Congress.

The publisher has no responsibility for the continued existence or accuracy of URLs for external or third-party internet websites referred to in this book, and does not guarantee that any content on such websites is, or will remain, accurate or appropriate.

With gratitude

Contents

Preface ix

Acknowledgments xv

A Note on Citations xvii

1: Prologue: *Das Gesamtgenie* 1
2: A Philosophical Age 11
3: Wagner as Philosopher 27
4: The Future that Failed 41
5: From *Siegfrieds Tod* to *Der Ring des Nibelungen* 59
6: *Das Rheingold*: Separation and Order 71
7: *Die Walküre*: Reasons of State 87
8. *Siegfried*: Stasis and Movement 99
9: *Götterdämmerung*: The Deed that Redeems the World 109
10: Epilogue: After Transcendence 123

Appendix: A Note on Schopenhauer 131

Works Cited 137

Index 143

Preface

> *Such mistakes are of course only possible in the case of a reader who substitutes his own ideas for those of the poet, while the simple-minded reader, perhaps unconsciously to himself, takes in the matter more easily, just as it is.*
> —Wagner to August Röckel, January 26, 1854

THIS BOOK DOES not look at Wagner's *Ring* cycle through concepts drawn from contemporary philosophy, as Philip Kitcher and Richard Schacht do in *Finding an Ending*.[1] Nor does it begin with the philosophers that Wagner was known to have read "and show in what ways their ideas got into Wagner's work," which was Bryan Magee's intention in *Wagner and Philosophy*.[2] Instead, it is a kind of experiment in interpretation. I begin with Wagner's own philosophy and then think through the *Ring* with the ideas that he himself had set out while preparing to write its text. I have made use of the secondary literature when it serves my argument, but the guiding thread is spun from Wagner's own words.

That is to say: I take Wagner seriously as a thinker, as a creator of philosophical theories rather than as a consumer of other people's. He was not a philosopher of the first rank, it is true, but his talents in that direction were substantial. Though he was strongly influenced by many of the better-known thinkers of his day, he developed his own theories on topics as diverse as humanity's place in the larger world, the limitations of human knowledge and the pitfalls of self-consciousness, the social function of art, the historical and cultural influences and constraints on artistic creativity, and the prospects for political transformation. More impressive than that was his ability to bring those ideas together into a single, surprisingly coherent world view.

Even if Wagner were not a great composer and dramatist the philosophy he formulated in those years would be worth investigating—but not all of it, unfortunately. He is notorious for his espousal of terrible ideas, most

---

1 Philip Kitcher and Richard Schacht, *Finding an Ending: Reflections on Wagner's Ring* (Oxford: Oxford University Press, 2004).
2 Brian Magee, *Wagner and Philosophy* (London: Penguin Books, 2001), 1.

notably an antisemitism that was extreme even by the standards of his age. That should not keep us from looking into what he wrote in his calmer moments. Wagner's antisemitism is not a necessary aspect of his overall philosophy or its inevitable outcome, and the very pathological nature of his obsession makes it relatively easy to separate it from his better ideas.

His "conversion" to the philosophy of Schopenhauer presents other difficulties, as much of his adopted philosophy was at odds with his own ideas, and for this and other reasons his thinking grew more inconsistent and even crankier as he aged. Whatever its problems, though, Wagner's earlier philosophy is an illuminating and arguably essential context for understanding his largest and perhaps greatest work, in which, as he wrote, his "entire philosophy of life … found its most perfect artistic expression."[3]

Wagner wrote the first sketches for what became *The Ring of the Nibelung* in 1848, in the time of European revolutions in which he played enough of a role to be forced into exile. Over the next few years, he wrote *Art and Revolution, The Artwork of the Future, Opera and Drama*, and his other major theoretical works. Soon after that he expanded and developed a libretto he had written in 1848 into the text of the four music dramas of the *Ring*, which he had privately printed in 1853.

Those five years were probably the most important in Wagner's career; it is when "Richard Wagner" emerged, the man whose ideas—hard as it may be for us to believe—were once as influential as his music. They cannot really be separated. *Der Ring des Nibelungen* is a theatrical work, not a philosophical text, but it gives dramatic and emotionally powerful expression to philosophical ideas.

The first part of this book is therefore devoted to the historical and intellectual context of Wagner's theories and to those theories themselves, and it touches on their political foundations and implications and how Wagner worked and reworked the text of the *Ring* after his part in the failed revolutions of 1848 and 1849. Through those revisions his Nibelung project grew not just in scale but in narrative and philosophical depth.

The early writings of Ludwig Feuerbach were a strong influence on this process, but I have also put Wagner's ideas alongside those of the philosopher Johann Gottlieb Fichte, whose productive period ran from 1792 to 1814. Richard Bell, who seems to have tracked down every imaginable source for Wagner's texts, concluded that Fichte "seems to have had little direct influence on the composer."[4] But Fichte was widely read

---

3   To Theodor Uhlig, May 31, 1852, *SL* 260.
4   Richard Bell, *The Theology of Wagner's Ring Cycle*, vol. I (Eugene, OR: Cascade Books, 2020), 177.

and discussed in Wagner's day, and Wagner famously picked up many of his ideas through conversation. His first and most important mentor, his uncle Adolf Wagner, who (in Wagner's words) "exercised no small influence on [his] development,"[5] had been a pupil of Fichte's and was an "intimate friend" of the Romantic poet and novelist Ludwig Tieck, who himself knew and was strongly influenced by the philosopher.[6] "Uncle Adolf," "a man whom the composer admired greatly throughout his life, and to whom he owed the decisive educational experiences of his youth,"[7] was a brilliant independent scholar, translator, and editor, whose interests encompassed writers as diverse as Byron and Sophocles (he translated both *Manfred* and *Oedipus Tyrannus*) and the heretic and proto-pantheist Giordano Bruno—in 1830 he edited and introduced (in Italian!) a pioneering set of Bruno's works. Wagner took delight in recalling long conversation-filled walks with his uncle and the philosophical discussions he heard at the home of this "extraordinarily interesting man."[8] Years later, he was to befriend another Fichtean, the revolutionary Mikhail Bakunin, who had translated one of Fichte's books into Russian, and though, like Adolf Wagner, Bakunin eventually fell under Hegel's influence, he remained deeply influenced by Fichte's religious ideas. With Bakunin, too, much of the relationship consisted of long walks and philosophical conversation.[9]

My argument, I should stress, is not that Wagner was a Fichtean, or that Fichte's ideas show up in the text of the *Ring*. It is Wagner's own philosophy which does. That philosophy, though, had taken shape in an intellectual world where Fichte was a significant presence, and Wagner's own ideas have a great many affinities with Fichte's popular writings and imply a world view which is far more Fichtean than it is anything else.

Those parallels are not just on matters we think of as metaphysical, either; the two writers' sociological and cultural analyses are very similar, as are their political hopes and their theories about the obstacles to

---

5   Richard Wagner, *My Life*, authorized translation (New York: Dodd, Mead & Co., 1911), 1.

6   *My Life*, 26. Tieck was a trusted associate of Fichte's into his first years in Berlin: Peter Neumann, *Jena 1800: The Republic of Free Spirits*, trans. Frisch (New York: Farrar, Straus and Giroux, 2022), 78. For one example of his engagement with Fichte's ideas see Alexander Mathäs, "Self-Perfection—Narcissism—Paranoia: Ludwig Tieck's 'Der blonde Eckbert,'" *Colloquia Germanica* 34, no. 3/4 (2001): 237–55.

7   Dieter Borchmeyer, *Richard Wagner: Theory and Theatre*, trans. Spencer (Oxford: Clarendon Press, 1991), 329.

8   *My Life*, 8, 66, and chapter 1, *passim*.

9   *My Life*, 470.

social transformation. This is unlikely to be a coincidence. Beyond any direct influence, however, Fichte's thinking is an invaluable guide to the concerns and aspirations of a world which is not as much like our own as we might think. It gives us the interpretive distance that, as Rilke said in quite another context, helps us to see Wagner "whole and against a wide sky."[10] What might seem to be fragmentary thoughts then turn out to be contributions to a conversation which, like any other conversation, depends for its intelligibility on shared presuppositions.

The philosophical content of the *Ring* cycle, though, is never conveyed directly. Nobody serves as a mouthpiece for Wagner's thoughts. Those thoughts are anything but absent, but they are shown and not spoken. Implicit in the situations with which we are presented, they also shape the characters' actions and their often-unexpected consequences. This cannot be demonstrated without an account of the four dramas of the cycle, and that is the function of the interpretive essays in the second part of this book. Here, too, I have tried to keep as close as possible to Wagner's own words, on the assumption that he tells his audience everything that they need to know.

He does so in compressed and allusive ways, however, and certain passages need unpacking as much as they need interpretation. They do make sense, and profound ones at that, but that sense becomes most evident in the combined light of Wagner's larger philosophical assumptions and the context of the work itself, which for Wagner encompassed not just music and poetry but dramatic action. What emerges from this inquiry is a different understanding of the *Ring* from many of those which are commonly held, but it is one which I hope will give readers some threads worth following as they find their own ways through Wagner's labyrinth.

Readers may wonder why I say so little about Schopenhauer, the philosopher with whom Wagner felt the most sympathy. The short answer is that Wagner had no awareness of Schopenhauer while he was working up the poem of the *Ring*. There is neither historical nor biographical justification for reading Schopenhauer into that text; what Wagner published in 1853 was effectively its final form, differing from the poem as he set it to music in only minor ways, and it was not until the fall of 1854 that a fellow refugee in Zurich gave him a copy of *The World as Will and Representation*, Schopenhauer's major work.[11]

---

10 Rainer Maria Rilke, *Rilke on Love and Other Difficulties*, trans. Mood (New York: Norton, 1975), 28.

11 Schopenhauer had only a cult following until the 1853 publication of an essay in the *Westminster Review*, and this fact supports the accuracy of Wagner's

Wagner soon announced that the philosopher had made clear what he had only intuited, often against his conscious intentions, but there is no reason to take this retrospective interpretation as authoritative and no need to try to reconcile the Schopenhauerian glosses with the text of the *Ring*. This tends to replace the work itself with a preconceived interpretation. Schopenhauer's philosophy can provide an interesting and perhaps even fruitful perspective on the *Ring*, but it has the same standing as any other set of ideas—Marxian, Jungian, queer theory, or what have you. It could not have had any formative influence on the poem itself, and thus, as one scholar writes, "it is unacceptable to trace the gigantic work or any of its so-called contradictions back to Schopenhauer."[12]

As the same writer goes on to say, however, "some legends are not so easily disposed of." Everyone who writes on Wagner and philosophy is likely to come up against what Wieland Wagner called "the old Schopenhauer story," and it could too easily look like an evasion if I passed it over in silence. For this reason I have written a short appendix on Schopenhauer, on Wagner's idiosyncratic understanding of his ideas, and on why the text of the *Ring* is best understood within the horizons of Wagner's reading and writing through 1853.

This book is meant both for scholars and for anyone with an interest in Wagner; I hope the former group will not be put off by its conversational tone and the latter will accept its many footnotes. While no philosophical training or historical background is necessary, it does assume a familiarity with the *Ring* itself. It is not an introduction to the cycle, and the chapters on the individual music dramas can best be appreciated by those who have seen them live or online, or at least listened to their scores with text in hand. A synopsis for each drama would not be sufficient, and any comprehensive one would probably overshadow the argument. Brief summaries of the action are easily found online; Chicago Lyric Opera's introduction is more than adequate.[13] But there is no substitute for first-hand experience with the *Ring* in performance. Wagner lived and breathed theater, and he makes his points visually and dramatically as well as through text and music. He judged his effects well, too; even modestly

---

recollection and also makes it highly unlikely that he would have had any knowledge of Schopenhauer's theories before that gift.

12 Hartmut Reinhardt, "Wagner and Schopenhauer," trans. Deathridge, in *The Wagner Handbook*, ed. Ulich Müller and Peter Wapniewski (Cambridge, MA: Harvard University Press, 1992), 294. Searching for Schopenhauer in the score itself present other problems, but these are outside the scope of the present work.

13 https://www.lyricopera.org/lyric-lately/beginners-guide-wagner-ring-cycle/.

scaled performances get those across, as do semi-staged productions like the well-regarded one from Opera North.

I make no apologies for the argument's occasional difficulties. The *Ring* is a profound work and it is hard to be profound and easy at the same time. This book may make it harder, but I believe it will also show that it is even more profound than it might appear the first time one falls under its spell. That has certainly been my experience.

Acknowledgments

I MIGHT NOT have written this book had my wife and I not gone to see *Das Rheingold* at the Wagner in Vermont festival in Brattleboro. We both felt from the beginning that Hugh Keelan had brought something extraordinary into being, but it was not until we spent a little time with him, his wife Jenna Rae, and much of the cast that we could see that besides deep musicianship and a strong sense of how the *Ring* could come together Hugh and Jenna had forged a genuine community, a circle of artists who learn from each other as much as they do from Wagner's daunting work. It was that community that drew me in, leading me to propose a lecture and then to develop the themes of that talk into this book. Those came to me almost unbidden, but it was Hugh who had opened me up to receive them.

The ideas had to be worked out, though, tested and researched and given life and form, and my wife Loret was witness, audience, and contributor to that process. She encouraged me, challenged me, and tried to rein in my enthusiasms until I had developed them into enthusiasms she could share. This would not have been the same book without her, and without her I would have taken far less pleasure in its composition.

Its main novelty, aside from its reliance on Wagner's own words, comes from taking the perspective of early German Idealism, Fichte's especially, and of the early German Romantics. It is only recently that Fichte has come to be seen as the challenging and influential figure that he was, and much of the credit for this important reevaluation has come from the North American Fichte Society, founded by the late Dan Breazeale and by Tom Rockmore. For the past seventeen years I have been able to present and share ideas at the biennial NAFS conferences, thanks in part to Dan's openness to ideas quite distant from his own, and a number of my Fichtean colleagues have helped me as I worked on this project; my appreciation goes out, in particular, to Yolanda Estes, David Wood, and Günter Zöller. Others, inside the academy and out, have listened, made suggestions, or simply encouraged me. Among those whose responses have kept my spirits up are Amy and Chris Capozziello, Mario Cerasuolo, Sarah Falkner, Franlee Frank, Ralph Locke, and Christopher

Satoor. Nicholas Kahn created the lovely image of Wagner in 1850 that is on the cover; I thank him, too.

Jim Walker, from Camden House, was far more than the editor every author dreams of, although he was that as well. The publication process has been a great pleasure, and I cannot say enough to thank him, copy editor Michael Wood, and Chris Adler-France.

I cannot close without mentioning one other person. I first heard the stories of the *Ring* from my late father, one of whose childhood treasures was an illustrated book he remembered as *The Story of Siegfried*. He would have loved to have talked this book over with me, and I wish that I would have had the opportunity to do that.

A Note on Citations

References to the text of the *Ring* are given as the initial letter of the original German title of the individual drama (omitting articles), act number, and line numbers, which can be found in Richard Wagner, *The Ring of the Nibelung*, translated by John Deathridge (Penguin Classics, 2018). I have consulted Deathridge's translation, as well as that of Stewart Spencer in Stewart Spencer and Barry Millington, *Wagner's Ring of the Nibelung: A Companion* (Thames & Hudson, 1993), but any uncredited translations are my own.

PW refers to *Richard Wagner's Prose Works*, translated by William Ashton Ellis. The University of Nebraska reprints are photo reproductions of the first editions, which were published at the end of the nineteenth century, and the volume numbers and pagination are the same in both. Titles without an author are all Wagner's work.

I have used and quoted the only modern translation of any of these texts, *The Artwork of the Future*, translated by Emma Warner (London: The Wagner Journal, 2013), and have supplied parallel citations to the Ellis translation.

SL refers to Stewart Spencer and Barry Millington, eds. and trans., *Selected Letters of Richard Wagner* (London: J. M. Dent, 1987).

1: Prologue: *Das Gesamtgenie*

THERE HAVE BEEN few if any composers with interests as varied as Wagner's, and certainly none has devoted so much time to weighing in on matters other than the purely musical. His *Gesamtkunstwerk* was to fuse poetry, music, dramatic action, dance, and the scenic arts, but even this was not enough for him; he read and wrote on history, geography, literary theory, aesthetics, religion, and philosophy, too, setting out his ideas in letters, articles, and books, and urging his favorite authors on his friends.

This sounds like the worst kind of dilettantism and intellectual overreaching. The composer Peter Cornelius, later a friend, had gently mocked him when he had his barber of Baghdad claim to be a comprehensive genius, *ein Gesamtgenie*. Later generations have been less kind on this score and not at all affectionate. Wagner's claims were so immodest, and his personal qualities so mixed—to put it mildly—that we almost want him to fail at least somewhere. What Auden saw in him sounds like a cosmic injustice: by what rights could such "an extraordinary genius" also be "an absolute shit?"[1]

Wagner's legion of adoring friends would have disagreed, but that combination may well be the truth, hard though it is to swallow. It is difficult to deny Wagner's greatness as a composer, though there are those who do, and his theatrical craft can hardly be gainsaid. He was indeed a master of the art of transition, and the music dramas are object lessons in structuring the ebb and flow of long works; even a merely competent performance will hold one's interest. Wagner as a poet stands in less repute. Thomas Mann saw both sides: "Purely as composition it is often bombastic, baroque, even childish; it has something majestically and sovereignly inept —side by side with such passages of absolute genius,

---

1 W. H. Auden, *The Dyer's Hand and Other Essays* (London: Faber and Faber, 1948), 48; quoted in Robert Craft, *Stravinsky: Chronicle of a Friendship* (Nashville, TN: Vanderbilt University Press, 1996), 530. Bryan Magee claimed that "in one of his volumes of essays" Auden wrote that Wagner "was perhaps the greatest genius that ever lived" (*Aspects of Wagner* [Oxford: Oxford University Press, 1988], 48). He does not give the source.

power, compression, primeval beauty, as disarm all doubt."[2] Whatever the literary quality of their texts, however, the dramas are clearly poetic; what happens in them is conveyed not just by the things that the words say outright, but also by what they do not say, by the imagery Wagner invokes and the metaphors he employs, and by their echoes of or contrasts with other images and metaphors. To be deaf to the poetic nature of these texts is not as grievous a weakness as a deafness to the music, but it takes away from the emotional content of the pieces all the same.

Wagner as philosopher is harder to defend, and many of those who take up this subject have often derided his abilities. The contemporary scholar Günter Zöller has pointed out that "most of his scholarly readers and academic interpreters ... chiefly refer to the theoretical assumptions and assertions implied by his artistic work—the textbooks [i.e., libretti] and the compositions of his operatic corpus. Where they consider his theoretical writings, they tend to treat their author as a dilettante thinker and regard his work as largely derivative of earlier authors."[3] Examples of this are easy to find. Michael Tanner insisted that all "attempts to turn Wagner into ... a philosopher in his own right" (this one included, I suppose) were "vain and misleading."[4] Mark Berry both sums up and dismisses Wagner's thinking—which he quotes only infrequently—as "agglomerative."[5] Sandra Corse, who argued for the presence of Hegelian ideas in the *Ring* cycle, indicates much the same through a footnote:

> Amerongen may be close to the truth when he suggests of Wagner, "In his guise as philosopher, he was a typical exponent of the nineteenth-century desire for a complete, self-contained view of the world, in which everything had its proper place and function. His writings form a half-baked mishmash of one particular brand of socialism and conservatism, Hellenism and Teutonism, antisemitism and vegetarianism, Proudhon, Hegel, Feuerbach, Gobineau and Schopenhauer."[6]

---

2   Thomas Mann, "Sufferings and Greatness of Richard Wagner," in Mann, *Essays of Three Decades*, trans. Lowe-Porter (New York: Knopf, 1948), 317.

3   Günter Zöller, "Romanticism as Modernism: Richard Wagner's 'Artwork of the Future,'" in *The Palgrave Handbook of German Romantic Philosophy*, ed. E. Millán Brusslan (London: Palgrave Macmillan, 2020), 597.

4   Michael Tanner, *Faber Pocket Guide to Wagner* (London: Faber and Faber, 2010), 189. He thought that "studies of the evolution of *The Ring*" were equally pointless.

5   Mark Berry, *Treacherous Bonds and Laughing Fire: Politics and Religion in Wagner's Ring* (London and New York: Routledge, 2006).

6   Sandra Corse, *Wagner and the New Consciousness: Language and Love in the "Ring"* (Rutherford, NJ: Fairleigh Dickinson Press, 1990), 193, n18.

Yet Nietzsche, who was not known to tolerate fools gladly, dedicated *The Birth of Tragedy* to Wagner, his "sublime predecessor,"[7] and even ten years after he broke off their friendship he could still write that Wagner had been the only person "up to now, or at least the first, who had any feeling for what I was up to."[8]

As Nicholas Vazsonyi writes, Wagner "was a keen observer of his own age and an artist who seemed to have grasped the long-term consequences of what we can simply call modernity."[9] He was able to theorize these, as well, but his manner of expressing his ideas created its own problems. While Zöller insists that Wagner deserves to be taken seriously "as a thinker in his own right—and as a philosophical thinker at that," he also sees some of the obstacles to that consideration. He concedes that "this neglect is due [in part] to the mode and manner of Wagner's theoretical writings, which tend to be written in a heavy-handed and belabored style."[10] It is also due to the scattered nature of his philosophical writings; the closest thing that Wagner came to a coherent expression of his fundamental ideas was in a long letter to his imprisoned friend and revolutionary comrade August Röckel.[11] Anyone who wants to present a coherent account of his philosophy must piece it together from the letters to Röckel, the book-length *Opera and Drama*, *The Artwork of the Future*, *Art and Revolution*, *A Communication to My Friends*, the sketches for *Jesus of Nazareth*, and many others.

What is more, these passages need to be read in the context of his philosophical milieu, not just the Left Hegelians but the German Idealists and even Kant. Wagner had first- or second-hand knowledge of much of their work, and he picked up and developed many of their central themes. As Zöller insists, a fair assessment of Wagner's work therefore requires "a distinctly philosophical perspective ... informed by the general outlook and the doctrinal specifics that form the background of his theoretical efforts," most of all "classical German philosophy in its vast extent."[12] This is a degree of expertise that is not common today, but something close to it is utterly necessary. It is too easy to miss the relevance and

---

7   Friedrich Nietzsche, "The Birth of Tragedy," in *Basic Writings of Nietzsche*, trans. Kaufmann (New York: Modern Library, 1968), 32.
8   Dieter Borchmeyer, "Wagner and Nietzsche," in *The Wagner Handbook*, 329–30.
9   Nicholas Vazsonyi, "Why Wagner?," in *The Cambridge Companion to Wagner's "Der Ring des Nibelungen,"* ed. Mark Berry and Nicholas Vazsonyi (Cambridge: Cambridge University Press, 2020), 8.
10   Zöller, "Romanticism as Modernism," 597.
11   See chapter 3, below.
12   Zöller, "Romanticism as Modernism," 597.

novelty of Wagner's thinking if one has no familiarity with the ideas and terminology of that philosophical tradition.

This is likely one reason that the letter to Röckel and other texts do not get the attention they deserve. Wagner is implicitly in dialogue with a number of important figures, but it needs some background knowledge to recognize this. For all these reasons, his own philosophy, aesthetics aside, seems to pass beneath the notice of most writers; specifically philosophical discussions are rarely quoted at any length and appear in most secondary texts only through a few fragments on the importance of love. Typical in many ways is Jean-Jacques Nattiez's *Wagner Androgyne*, which argues, as this book does, for the essential interconnection between the *Ring* and Wagner's theoretical works,[13] but then discusses those works as if they were entirely concerned with art and society, completely ignoring Wagner's analysis of the fundamental problems which art and social practices both seek to resolve.

"In the beginning were the Greeks," Nattiez writes,[14] but in fact Wagner did not start there. He started with the emergence of self-awareness. *The Artwork of the Future*, one of the very texts Nattiez describes, insists on its first page that "error [was] the first expression of consciousness," born in the "moment we began to develop as human beings and to break away from our unconscious, animal existence as children of nature to wake to conscious life."[15] We begin with a fall, and the Greeks come along later.

But why should this bother us? The music dramas speak for themselves. They seem at first blush to resist the kind of disinterested consideration that we associate with philosophy. When the curtain falls on the frenetic close of Act One of *Die Walküre* we do not immediately think of the propriety of brother-sister incest, and it is probably better that way. The very brilliance of Wagner's theatrical craftsmanship, his unparalleled command of musical flow, his ability to surpass one overwhelming climax with another one even more overwhelming, and the variety of color and the sheer volume of sound that he could draw from his expanded orchestra, all contribute to a sense of being carried away, of being overmastered by a force that is not our own and which seems to silence all of our qualms and critical faculties.

---

13   Jean-Jacques Nattiez, *Wagner Androgyne*, trans. Spencer (Princeton, NJ: Princeton University Press, 1993), 8–11.
14   Nattiez, *Wagner Androgyne*, 13.
15   Richard Wagner, *The Artwork of the Future*, trans. Warner (London: The Wagner Journal, 2013), 11, *PW* I, 70.

But thinking comes back in soon enough. Brian Magee suggests that "Wagner's music expresses, as does no other art, repressed and highly charged contents of the psyche, and that this is the reason for its uniquely disturbing effect."[16] But this is only part of the story. Wagner's work is disturbing because it raises difficult questions. When the initial shock of his unsurpassable climaxes passes we do find ourselves thinking about why characters acted as they did, what the dramas might mean, and how they might connect with our own concerns and predicaments. Aspects of the psyche or not, Wagner's characters have ideas about serious issues, and they act on those ideas and spend what to some seems an inordinate amount of time discussing them. The very dramatic situations in which they find themselves depict important social, historical, and religious problems; even on the surface, much of the *Ring* self-evidently concerns Wotan's attempts to maintain a contractually based world-order in the face of unlimited power. And if we dig more deeply into the texts, if we consider more deeply what has passed before us and what we have heard, we may find that Wagner has presented us with a vision that allows us no simple or comforting answers to the problems it touches on.

Few other operas present the same challenges. As great as Verdi's operas are—and they are unsurpassable in their own way—his interests were generally centered on emotional intensity and conflict; his characters are humanly affecting as Wagner's rarely are, but we relate to them directly, as suffering individuals. Aida is torn between her status as a foreign captive and her love for Radames, Egypt's general, a plight made more painful by the concealed fact that she is the daughter of the enemy's king. The Egyptian-Ethiopian war moves the plot along but is never thematized; what counts is not the justice of the Ethiopian cause but its effectiveness in highlighting the impossibility of Aida's position, which she embraces and resolves by remaining in Egypt and offering her dying moments to comfort the man she loves. We leave a Verdi opera moved by the pathos of the story and the people caught up in it, but we rarely feel the need to go beyond that.

With Wagner we do. We recognize Verdi's characters, they are people like us and their world is our world, but Wagner's characters stand at one remove from the lives we lead and their worlds reflect on ours as from an alien perspective. Magee called the dramas "animated textbooks of psychoanalysis."[17] George Bernard Shaw, with perhaps clearer

---

16 Magee, *Aspects of Wagner*, 39.
17 Magee, *Aspects of Wagner*, 36. He excepted *Die Meistersinger*.

insight, saw the *Ring* as an allegory of capitalism.[18] Robert Donington read it as story of inner self-realization in accord with Jungian depth psychology. I doubt that any of these is entirely accurate, and certainly none is really comprehensive. The *Ring*, more than any other work of art in the Western canon, seems endlessly interpretable. But that is because it demands interpretation. It is a puzzle, which it would not be if it showed us women and men just like ourselves.

This brings us back to Wagner, the man of the theater. "My only language is Art," he wrote,[19] and the long history of the composition of the poem of the *Ring* bears this out.[20] He knew from the beginning that Brünnhilde was to join Siegfried on his funeral pyre and that this would set off some kind of cataclysm. Such a stage image was hardly original. It echoed the fiery climax of his early grand opera *Rienzi*, and it was uncomfortably close to the orgies of scenic destruction in Meyerbeer's operas which he was famously to deride as "effects without causes." Wagner was surely aware of this, but he was convinced that his ending was different from the French claptrap it only superficially resembled, and he was determined to find a cause for his effect.

It would be uncharitable to think of this as a rationalization. Wagner had a vision of how the *Ring* had to end, but it took a great deal of thought and revision to understand what had to perish and why. In a real sense the entirety of the *Ring* unfurls from that original vision. As he told Röckel:

> That in us, which is essentially and fundamentally our own, are not our conceptions but our intuitions. These, however, are so inalienably a part of our being, that we can never wholly express them, never adequately communicate them. ... [H]e himself feels in the presence of his work, if it is true Art, that he is confronted by a riddle, about which he too might have illusions, just as another might.[21]

This is not an extraordinary experience in the creation of a work of art, but it is hardly unknown in philosophy, either. Luther said he suddenly understood justification by faith while sitting in a privy, and his later elaborations of this seminal idea often make scatological allusions to the Devil. The philosopher Johann Gottlieb Fichte, whom we shall encounter in the next chapter, had a moment of insight while warming himself

---

18 This is the theme of *The Perfect Wagnerite*.
19 Richard Wagner, *Letters to August Roeckel*, trans. Sellar (Bristol: J. W. Arrowsmith, 1897), 153 (August 23, 1856), *SL* 358.
20 See chapter 5, below.
21 34 *Letters to August Roeckel*, 146–47 (August 23, 1856), *SL* 356–57.

by a stove. What happened, he said much later, was that suddenly God was looking through his eyes and he was looking through God's, and for the twenty years of philosophizing that were left to him he continued to unfold and look more deeply into the vision that he felt he had received. Wagner's process was part of this tradition.

When we sit down after a performance of one of the *Ring* dramas and think and talk about what it could be about, why Wotan needs to build Valhalla, why Brünnhilde defies him, why she and Siegfried go so tragically astray, and of course why it all has to end in fire and flood, we are doing much the same thing that Wagner did in the long gestation of his grandest work. The *Ring* is a record of its own making, much as a Jackson Pollock painting is, and it is most deeply understood if we can walk into the finished product and share in that creative process.

Where Wagner's dramas are concerned, then, philosophy is not merely an interesting or intellectually enjoyable extra. It is a way of contemplating those works, of turning them over in our minds and seeing the hidden sinews and blood vessels that make what happens both necessary and illuminating. It brings our lives and the lives of the characters and their creator together in an intricate dance of meaning and association. One can enjoy Wagner without a whit of philosophical training or interest. To go down the rabbit-hole of Wagner's philosophical environment and his own, surprisingly interesting contributions to the tradition of classical German philosophy brings us closer to those works, though, and lets us share in the creative process that produced them.

Seeing them in context also makes them richer, stranger, and more of a challenge to our ordinary ways of seeing things. This seems a bit like a paradox. It is a common practice these days, especially in opera houses, to update stage works, subjecting them to often well-deserved criticism for racist or sexist attitudes and presenting them in ways that reflect or evoke contemporary problems or concerns. Directors want to make us think, not just enjoy, and to do this they draw upon a wide range of theatrical techniques and startle us with the unexpected. Yuval Sharon, engaged by the Metropolitan Opera for a new staging of the *Ring*, has said that he wants opera, all of it, to be "deeply engaged with society and with our time and not removed, not distanced, and not in any way hermetically sealed from the way that the world is currently operating."[22]

It is hard to disagree with his ambitions, but such well-intentioned efforts often backfire and make the works less relevant, not more. The

---

22 https://operawire.com/q-a-yuval-sharon-on-his-new-book-a-new-philosophy-of-opera-the-upcoming-ring-cycle/.

problem with politically or socially informed *Regietheater*, with "modernizing" works or stripping away anything that smacks of the traditional, is not so much that we set ourselves up as critics of the works and ideas of others. It is that we do not subject our own ideas to the same critique. We quite rightly take Enlightenment thinkers to task when they write as if all people and all cultures were identical at heart and should be weighed by the "universal" logic and values of white, privileged, male, late-eighteenth-century European Christians. It is harder for us to see that by turning the characters of the past into recognizable contemporary types with recognizable interests and motivations we, too, make everyone into duplicates of ourselves, and that that we, too, issue our judgments from what we think of as universal logic and values. If we leave our descendants a world which permits them the leisure of study they are likely to find that our own stance was as limited and one-sided as those of Voltaire, Kant, Fichte, and Wagner. Our universal nature may look as parochial as theirs and our values just as much a mixture of laudable ideals and self-satisfaction.

Trying to see the works of the past on their own terms, though, can force us to set our own ideas aside. This is especially fruitful in the case of Wagner. It may even be necessary, because thinking through complex ideas was part of his working process, because his ideas were not always our own, and most of all, perhaps, because he was not inclined to take ideas, or instincts and emotions, for granted, trying instead to uncover some underlying problem or activity which gave rise to those ideas, emotions, and actions. In his day, at least, this was the task of philosophy: to look beneath the surface.

We do this less often than we might think, and many of our explanations, such as those offered by evolutionary psychology, do little but affirm the way things are. We say that we humans long to feel part of something larger than ourselves, and we assume that this is something inherent in our nature. We then put that idea to work as an explanation for religion, for sex, for eating or drinking together, for nationalism, warfare, fascism, consumerism, a taste for psychedelic drugs, and for much more.

We would not feel that longing unless we felt confined within our selves in the first place, but this, too, appears to need no explanation. Where else could we start from if not from the inner lives of individuals? It seems obvious to us that we are independent beings who find or make our inner and therefore authentic natures, and who pursue our private dreams while negotiating the demands and temptations of the world outside. Our insatiable yearning for meaning and connection is simply the sad or even tragic downside of our freedom.

When we look at Wagner's dramas in that light, we see characters responding in their various ways to the temptations of power, the desire for recognition, acceptance, and love, and the fear of death; those are the issues that count for isolated subjects making their way through an indifferent or hostile world. But for Wagner, and for most of the philosophers of his time and place, those seemed to beg the question. They wanted to know *why* we feel ourselves to be alone in the world, *why* we think that we are not part of anything larger than ourselves. Fichte and his successors assumed that a web of activity and force gave rise to everything: horses, rocks, Wagner's beloved dogs, bedbugs, planets, forests, oceans, and—most importantly—everything that we feel, think, and do. They thought of this process in different ways and gave it different names, but they all agreed that we can never be separated from its activity, and indeed that we are active within it, making it and shaping it as well as being made and shaped by it. Somehow, though, we have trouble seeing this. Something in the nature of self-consciousness itself, they thought, obscures the roots of our own being. That is where our estrangement begins.

Wagner, as we saw, spoke of "error as the first moment of consciousness." He was putting into his own words what was perhaps the fundamental insight of Fichte and the philosophers and poets who came after him: that life is a seamlessly collaborative activity that we can experience only in the confrontational form of self and other. This theme is always in the background when he treats issues of love or power, and it is reflected in the structure and movement of the *Ring* and the conflicts and struggles of its major characters. Seeing his dramas in this context makes sense of some otherwise puzzling events and illuminates aspects of the cycle that might otherwise go without notice.

Wagner's engagement with classical German philosophy, then, is much more than a dilettantish desire to stick his finger in every pie. It helped him plumb depths few other artists have even tried to explore, and to grasp and express matters so foundational that they do their work without anyone's notice. Out of that engagement came not only "sustained politico-philosophical thinking about human social existence under conditions of modernity,"[23] as Zöller says, but deep and challenging insights into the personal and emotional cost of a certain way of life, not just the life of Wotan's age or Wagner's but of ours as well. To take up those challenges, though, we need some sense of the intellectual world in which Wagner moved and to which he contributed. We need to talk philosophy.

---

23   Zöller, "Romanticism as Modernism," 598.

2: A Philosophical Age

In Wagner's day philosophy was not the specialized and even arcane practice it is today. Members of the educated public—not as large a group as it is now, but not at all negligible—aspired to stay up to date with important philosophical ideas and systems. In Germany, especially, philosophy was a normal topic in drawing rooms, coffee houses, and even taverns, and there was an entire genre of "popular philosophy" books; Haydn, who was no intellectual, owned one of those. There was nothing unusual or surprising in Wagner's interest, then. He stood out only through his seriousness and abilities.

Interest in philosophy was broad because philosophical ideas and systems met a widespread and genuine need. For more than a millennium and a half European civilization had been held together by an intricate weave of stories, images, and explanations that centered on the tenets of the Catholic church. That was the foundation for the sense people made of their own lives and of the public life of what people tended to call "Christendom." It hardly eliminated conflict, but it provided a common basis for arguing over significant issues. All parties shared the assumption that some resolution could be achieved, if not through human sagacity and agency then through the providential designs of an all-powerful and beneficent deity. That pleasant illusion did not survive the shock of the Reformation, the hardening of intellectual positions with the Counter-Reformation, and, worst of all, the endless and brutal wars of the sixteenth and seventeenth centuries, which had roots in environmental and economic crises as well but were carried out under the banner of religion. After this "European Crisis of Conscience" Christendom looked like a phantasm, not a reality.

The need for a unifying discourse survived; it was even intensified, thanks to the Protestant stress on individual responsibility and explicit belief and the Catholic "Counter-Reformation." Thoughtful and well-intentioned Germans and other Europeans wanted to know what kind of order could be made of their world and, more intimately, what kind of beings they were, what their lives counted for, how they were to live, and what they should strive for. They rarely abandoned their faith in the Christian God, and most of them continued to take communion and listen patiently to the sermons preached every Sunday, but more and more of them looked to human reason for answers, and the people who worked hardest to provide those answers were the philosophers. Philosophy was no longer the handmaid of theology. It had declared its independence and even tried to take the place of religion, establishing essential truths through rationality instead of revelation.

Here, for example, is Fichte in 1790, at the time an impoverished and underemployed tutor who had worked unhappily in a series of wealthy households:

> I have been living in a new world ever since reading [Kant's] *Critique of Practical Reason*. Propositions which I thought could never be overturned have been overturned for me. Things have been proven to me which I thought could never be proven—for example, the concept of absolute freedom, the concept of duty, etc.—and I feel all the happier for it. It is unbelievable how much respect for mankind and how much strength this system gives us![1]

Four years later, when through his own brilliance and some improbable happenstances he had been called to Jena and the most prestigious chair of philosophy in all of Germany, Fichte's own ideas were received with equal enthusiasm. He wrote to his wife:

> Last Friday I delivered my first public lecture. The largest auditorium in Jena was too small. The entire entrance hall and courtyard were filled; people were standing on tables, benches, and each other's heads.[2]

As many as five hundred people were soon crowding in to hear his talks, which were shortly published in book form.

Wagner was part of this world. He was born in 1813, a year before Fichte died, and came of age in the years right after Hegel's death in 1831, but his philosophical sympathies were those of an earlier generation—that of his uncle Adolf, the follower of Hegel's who had studied under Fichte and who was a formative influence in his intellectual development. As Dieter Borchmeyer wrote, "Wagner was fond of denying his century"; he wished he had been born ten years earlier, and in 1847 he

---

1 Johann Gottlieb Fichte, "Fragment of a letter to Weisshuhn, August–September 1790," in Fichte, *Early Philosophical Writings*, ed. and trans. Breazeale (Ithaca, NY: Cornell University Press, 1988), 357.

2 Quoted in Fichte, *Early Philosophical Writings*, 19. The letter was dated May 26, 1794.

sought out Ludwig Tieck, the friend of Fichte's and Adolf Wagner's who was the longest-lived of the circle of Jena Romantics.[3] Wagner recalled that Tieck "welcomed him almost as a friend, and [he] found [his] long talks with him exceedingly valuable."[4]

"The course of philosophy runs from Ionia to Jena," said Franz Rosenzweig, and Kant and his immediate successors came up with ideas that were essential to Wagner's world view and remain vital today. These can be fiendishly difficult, and it would be a fool's errand to present them in a book this size, let alone a single chapter, but there is luckily no need to do this. Wagner, like most of the rest of the educated public of his day, did not try to grapple with rebarbative texts like Fichte's *Foundations of the Entire "Wissenschaftslehre"* or Hegel's *Logic.* The journals and books written for a lay audience presented the leading ideas of the big-name philosophers in manageable, even simplified form. Fichte himself published books which he hoped would reach the general public, and Hegel's successors and critics, taking sides in an increasingly uneasy continent, worked hard to persuade and enlist support from ordinary readers. To appreciate Wagner's philosophical background, then, it is necessary only to trace out a few major themes.[5]

The "classical German philosophy" that Zöller refers to begins with Kant. We tend to think of Kant as engaged in two different tasks, and these are often studied or analyzed separately. He is read as a theorist of knowledge, arguing that we know only appearances, not things in themselves, and showing how we convert the stream of sense-impressions into objects and events that we can grasp and think about. He called this theory "transcendental idealism," by which he meant to highlight the human role in shaping experience. But he is also studied as a moral philosopher, a proponent of a rule based ("deontological") ethics, who argued that our acts were moral only if and when we followed the "categorical imperative" that we must treat each person "as an end and not a means."[6]

For Kant, however, these were two sides of the same coin, and he had set out to limit the realm of knowledge to make way for a "rational

---

3   Borchmeyer, *Richard Wagner: Theory and Theatre,* xv.

4   *My Life,* 420. Wagner claimed that he first read about Tannhäuser in one of Tieck's books, although it is more likely that his first acquaintance with the tale came from Heine. *A Communication to My Friends, PW* I, 311; Borchmeyer, *Richard Wagner: Theory and Theatre,* 216–18.

5   This discussion may nonetheless be difficult, and readers who find it unnecessarily so may skip to chapter 3 with little loss to the overall argument.

6   This is the best-known of his three formulations of the imperative.

faith."[7] He allowed that everything that we saw in the realm of appearances looked to be fully determined. We, too, appeared to be without free will, always pushed from one act to another by our bodily and emotional inclinations. But this was just another appearance, and we knew something about what we were in ourselves that showed us that this appearance was deceptive. We knew that we were subject to the moral law, which required us to set aside private interests and inclinations and treat everyone equally. And since we could choose to follow that law or ignore it, our will must be free.

That was not something that we could establish scientifically, because science lived and died in the world of appearances, but it was absolutely true nonetheless. For an era unsure of revelation this was a liberating message. Kant showed us that we were free beings with the power to make ourselves and our world and with the obligation to take up that work. Fichte was driving that point home even in his first lectures: "It is unkind to censure men and to mock them bitterly without telling them how they could improve. Act! Act! That is what we are here for."[8]

But this led to other questions. Was there any connection among the different parts of Kant's philosophy? Could we know anything about reality besides the fact of human freedom? Could we have any insight into who and what we are? Fichte worried away at these problems, and from his moment of vision at the stove he thought he know how to solve them.

He did not come up with some special kind of intuition or some different way of knowing. He looked at how a self-conscious being could know anything at all, and he realized that this begins with a split. To know something is to hold it at arm's length, to treat it as an object. But the world is not made up of natural objects and natural subjects that go around gathering knowledge about those things. The separation between subject and object is something that we make ourselves. It is a human creation. We break the flow of sensation into things that we see, smell, feel and can know, on the one hand, and an I or a self that does the seeing, smelling, feeling, thinking, and knowing on the other.[9]

---

7   Immanuel Kant, *Critique of Pure Reason*, trans. Kemp-Smith (London: Macmillan & Sons, 1933), 29 (B xxx).

8   Johann Gottlieb Fichte, "Some Lectures concerning the Scholar's Vocation," in Fichte, *Early Philosophical Writings*, 184.

9   The self, of course, seems to be there for the finding, but that commonsense view falls apart once we look at it carefully; as Dieter Henrich showed, self-reference is riddled with paradoxes: "Fichte's Original Insight," in *Contemporary German Philosophy, Volume 1*, ed. Darrel E. Christensen, et al. (University Park: Pennsylvania State University Press, 1982), 19–23.

It would be a mistake to think that Fichte was advocating individualism here. He was trying to show just the opposite. The self is a fiction. It is a necessary one; we had to imagine ourselves to be standing at one remove from the world before we could think about it and, indeed, think about ourselves. But we have to recognize that this process is exactly why we can never see ourselves as we really are. This means that truth lies outside of knowledge, and the only way we can know ourselves and know right from wrong is through feeling. For Fichte, this explained and justified Kant's decision to limit knowledge and make room for faith.

In his *System of Ethics*, widely read through much of the nineteenth century, Fichte wrote that individuality begins when "the I tears itself away—from itself—and puts itself forward as something self-sufficient."[10] In his early works he said nothing about what it was that the self tears itself away from. This was a risky topic. We fool ourselves if we think that we know anything about reality as it really is, and though Fichte was deeply religious he refused to say anything about God, because "by comprehending something it ceases to be God; and every supposed concept of God is necessarily that of an idol."[11] Reality was pure action, not a "thing" at all, and he insisted that "something that is stable, at a standstill, and dead can never enter the orbit of what I call philosophy."[12]

That pure action is what gives rise to everything that we sense or know, however, and when Fichte wrote for the general public he was willing to talk about the activity itself—though not where it came from. His "popular works" had broad appeal; the English translations stayed in print for decades and went through four editions, for example, and they were read, much as he intended, as religious or spiritual in character. In the best-known of these, *The Vocation of Humanity*, he portrayed the creative and ever-changing movement of reality as the "one life" of the divine:

---

10 Johann Gottlieb Fichte, *The System of Ethics According to the Principles of the Wissenschaftslehre*, trans. and ed. Breazeale and Zöller (Cambridge: Cambridge University Press, 2005), 37.

11 Johann Gottlieb Fichte, "Juridical Defense," trans. Bowman, in *J. G. Fichte and the Atheism Dispute (1798–1800)*, ed. Yolanda Estes and Curtis Bowman (Farnham/Burlington, VT: Ashgate, 2010), 179.

12 Johann Gottlieb Fichte, "From a Private Letter," trans. Bowman, in *J. G. Fichte and the Atheism Dispute*, 255. Much of Fichte's more technical writing concerns the processes whereby we render this activity as the interaction of stable objects (ourselves included) in space and time, but this aspect of his idealism was not widely understood in his day and did not play a major role in the popular works we are concerned with here.

[T]his Life, clothed to the eye of the mortal with manifold sensible forms, flows forth through me, and throughout the immeasurable universe of Nature. Here it streams as self-creating and self-forming matter through my veins and muscles, and pours out its abundance into the tree, the plant, the grass. ... There, in free play, it leaps and dances as spontaneous activity in the animal, and manifests itself in each new form as a new, peculiar, self-subsisting world:—the same power which, invisibly to me, moves and animates my own frame. Everything that lives and moves follows this universal impulse, this one principle of all motion, which, from one end of the universe to the other, guides the harmonious movement;—in the animal without freedom; in me, from whom in the visible world the motion proceeds although it has not its source in me, with freedom.[13]

It is significant that the title Fichte chose for this book was borrowed from a popular religious tract.

That is the something-larger that we long to connect with. The irony is that we are never apart from it; it is simply inaccessible within the subject-object structure of self-consciousness. We cannot say anything about it, but we can, as it were, hear its music and dance with it. To embrace its universal movement we simply need to abandon our efforts to understand things intellectually, set aside the selves that we make for ourselves, and let go of the illusion that we are all pursuing separate and independent lives.[14]

Fichte argued in his *System of Ethics* that the truly good person is not someone who adopts better rules for her life or who has better values. What makes her ethical is that she does not act for herself at all. This gives vivid life to the Kantian idea of the moral law, which is no longer an obligation imposed on us but a call to self-realization. When someone acts ethically she leaves behind everything individual about herself and becomes what she truly is: a "pure presentation" of the life that we all share. In such a moment she feels herself, correctly, to be at one with the activity which makes and unmakes all things.

The religious person, too, is unattached to her individuality, and this frees her from thinking of it as her own identity. She knows that she and all others are nothing more than masks of god, moments in the infinite life of the divine, and her life becomes blessedness and revelation. "In that which the Holy Man does, lives, and loves," Fichte wrote, "God

---

13 Johann Gottlieb Fichte, *The Vocation of Man*, in *The Popular Works of Johann Gottlieb Fichte*, trans. Smith (London: Trübner & Co. [4th ed.] 1889), vol. I, 475.

14 Fichte's demand that we act without ego saves his position from an emotive irrationalism.

appears ... in his own, immediate, and efficient Life; ... [God] is that which he who is devoted to him does."[15]

We are not puppets in god's hands, though, any more than we are independent, self-directed individuals. Human freedom and agency are real, but they are shared. Fichte was always a political radical, and his politics came directly out of his metaphysics. We are all equal participants in that one life, he taught, with everyone making and remaking each other's lives in an open-ended conversation of words and deeds. This was inconsistent with anything but complete human equality:

> [W]here the petty, narrow self of mere individual personality is merged in the more comprehensive unity of the social constitution, each man truly loves every other as himself,—as a member of this greater self which now claims all his love, and of which he himself is no more than a member, capable of participating only in a common gain or in a common loss.[16]

Such a commonwealth could come into being because it grew out of the activity that forms and transforms everything. The "mysterious union" in which "each soul unfolds itself only through its fellows,"[17] would not hold anyone or anything in place. It was all movement, all change and development, and a truly free society would be shaped by that activity instead of telling us what we should think or do. As the contemporary philosopher Dieter Henrich noted, Fichte and many of his contemporaries were committed to "a rationality that, without a fundamental orientation towards the contents of the world or toward eternally fixed, given rules, spontaneously generates ways of organizing thought and the dynamics of rational life."[18]

Among those contemporaries was the circle of Romantic poets and thinkers, Tieck included, who, by an extraordinary coincidence, were Fichte's neighbors in Jena. The poet Novalis, Tieck's close friend and one of the most philosophically gifted of that group, put the problem of self-consciousness in a nutshell: he complained that "we seek the absolute

---

15   Johann Gottlieb Fichte, *The Way to the Blessed Life*, in *The Popular Works of Johann Gottlieb Fichte*, trans. Smith (London: John Chapman, 1859), vol. II, 374.
16   Fichte, *The Way to the Blessed Life*, 435–36.
17   Fichte, *The Way to the Blessed Life*, 476.
18   Dieter Henrich, "The French Revolution and German Philosophy," trans. Martin and Bernecker in Henrich, *Aesthetic Judgment and the Moral Image of the World: Studies in Kant* (Stanford, CA: Stanford University Press, 1992), 91.

everywhere and only ever *find* things."[19] This led the Romantics to experiment with "symphilosophy" and a poetry of fragments, engaging in open-ended dialogues to overcome the inevitable limitations of our existence as individuals. "One person's poesy must be limited precisely because it is his own," wrote Friedrich Schlegel. "The spirit cannot bear this, because it knows, without knowing it, that no human being is merely a human being, but rather can and should be, really and in truth, all of humanity as well. Therefore a person keeps going outside of himself, ever certain of finding himself again, in order to seek and find the completion of his innermost being in the depths of a stranger."[20]

Elsewhere in Germany, in 1796 or 1797, the young Hegel wrote or copied a short text, from which only two pages survive. (We do not know if this was his work alone or involved his former seminary-school roommates Schelling and Hölderlin.) It is now called the "Earliest Program for a System of German Idealism," and it called for "a new mythology ... a mythology of *reason*. ... [E]nlightened and unenlightened must shake hands, mythology must become philosophical, and the people reasonable, and philosophy must become mythological in order to make the philosophers sensuous. Then eternal unity will reign among us. No longer the blind trembling of the people before their sages and priests. Only then will we find the *equal* cultivation *of all* powers, those of the single person as well as of all individuals. ... [U]niversal freedom and equality of the sprits will reign!"[21] Little of this would make sense unless all of humanity shared one life and one root.

Human progress was no illusion. It expressed and responded to the spontaneity and creativity of that underlying reality. But it was also limited and put in danger at times by the fact that it was made by fallible beings trapped in the inevitable illusions of self-consciousness. No amount of philosophizing could keep us from seeing ourselves as individuals, and as a result we were always a step or two behind the creativity of what was real. We could grasp it only through images. The divine life, wrote Fichte, "never [reveals itself to us as] a fixed and known entity, but as something

---

19 Novalis, *Philosophical Writings*, trans. Stoljar (Albany: SUNY Press, 1997), 23 (originally published in the collection *Pollen*).

20 Friedrich Schlegel, "Dialogue on Poesy," trans. Michel and Oksiloff, in *Theory as Practice: A Critical Anthology of Early German Romantic Writings*, ed. Jochen Schulte-Sasse et al. (Minneapolis: University of Minnesota Press, 1997), 181.

21 "Earliest Program for a System of German Idealism," trans. Mittman and Strand, in *Theory as Practice*, 73. The authorship of this 1796 text is still contested, but the most common view is that it is a collective text transcribed or summarized by Hegel.

that is to be; and after it has become what it was to be, it will reveal itself again to all eternity as something that is to be."[22]

Like the Torah in the Talmudic tradition, everything was in the hands of humanity, and human life was an eternal striving to make itself into the moving image of the life of the divine. This grounded Fichte's intense moral and political activism. It was a compelling vision to his students at Jena and to writers as various as Thomas Carlyle and Ralph Waldo Emerson. To his great successor Hegel, though, it was a mistake. In his first published book he criticized Fichte for placing a gap at the center of his theorizing. According to Hegel, Fichte was never able to connect or unify his Ego-subject with the Absolute. His "Reason" became mere intellect, the Absolute was understood "only in the form in which it appears to philosophical reflection" and "finitude and opposition are not removed."[23]

This misses Fichte's point. Finitude and opposition are not characteristics of what is ultimately real, so they do not have to be "removed." They seem to exist only because they characterize how the world must look if it is to be seen at all. But the criticism does help explain Hegel's own philosophy, because he brought finitude and opposition into the same process as infinity and unification. In his system the split which makes self-consciousness possible is itself the work of the Absolute, or Spirit.

Hegel's "absolute idealism" is head-spinning, but it is not necessary to follow his arguments in detail to see what his theories meant to the general public.[24] He portrayed all the horrors and joys of individual and collective life as moments in the perpetual self-development and self-revelation of a protean creativity:

---

22 Johann Gottlieb Fichte, *Addresses to the German Nation*, trans. Kelly (New York: Harper & Row, 1968), 38.

23 G. W. F. Hegel, *The Difference Between Fichte's and Schelling's System of Philosophy*, trans. Harris and Walter Cerf (Albany: SUNY Press, 1977), 81.

24 What Hegel did, in simple terms, was to ground his system on self-negation, not self-identity. The moment of creation, not in the Biblical sense but the logical one, is the Absolute's negation of itself. But the second moment is the negation of that negation, and even though this second moment is as negative as the first it makes that first moment into something determinate, something real; we cannot negate something that doesn't exist. This is the root of the famous Hegelian dialectic, which is far more subtle than the three-step of thesis-antithesis-synthesis often associated with him. It is an ascending spiral in which activity creates its own negation, but then resolves the conflict in a way that negates and preserves the oppositions that its own movement has generated. This and other topics in this chapter are considered in more detail in my *Enlightenment Interrupted: The Lost Moment of German Idealism and the Reactionary Present* (London and New York: Zero Books, 2014).

> Spirit gains its truth only through finding itself within absolute rupture. Spirit is that power not as a positive, which turns away from the negative, as when we say of something that it is nothing or false, and having thus finished with it we turn to something else; rather, spirit is that power only in so far as it looks the negative in the face and dwells in it. This dwelling is the magic force that converts the negative into being.[25]

The creative movement of Spirit was also destructive. But the opposite was also true; by negating the negative it was affirmation, an almost Buddhist lightness in the recognition that the coming-to-be and passing-away of all things was simply Spirit as it made and unmade itself:

> Appearance is coming-to-be and vanishing ... and constitutes the actuality and movement of the life of truth. The truth is thus the Bacchanalian whirl in which no member is not drunk; and because each one vanishes immediately upon its separation it is also transparent and simple rest.[26]

Even if one could not follow the theory behind it, there was great appeal in the thought that the world was moved by and lived in Spirit, as were we ourselves, and indeed that the only thing that kept life from being the full revelation of the divine was our own ignorance of that fact.[27] Everything had its place, everything was capable of being understood, and reason was present wherever you looked.

Hegel's system was one of the grand accomplishments of a century that delighted in big plans, every bit as ambitious as Wagner's *Ring* cycle and just as open to criticism. It was nowhere near as bulletproof as it looked. How could we know that the divine purpose had really been realized? Were we really in possession of absolute knowledge, the knowledge Hegel claimed to have brought us to grasp at the end of his *Phenomenology*? And even if it was, what was that knowledge? Was it the final truth, which would bring history to an end—as the latter-day Hegelian Francis Fukuyama thought for a while—or was it the truth of one way of life, something retrospective, which could tell us nothing about what could or should develop from there?

Late in his life Hegel seemed to opt for the latter:

---

25 G. W. F. Hegel, *Faith and Knowledge*, trans. Cerf and Harris (Albany, SUNY Press, 1977), 129.
26 G. W. F. Hegel, *The Phenomenology of Spirit*, Preface, § 47. My translation.
27 G. W. F. Hegel, *Hegel's Logic, being Part One of the Encyclopedia of the Philosophical Sciences*, trans. Wallace (1873; reprint, Oxford: Clarendon Press, 1973), § 212, 274.

A further word on the subject of *issuing instructions* on how the world ought to be: philosophy, at any rate, always comes too late to perform this function. ... When philosophy paints its grey in grey, a shape of life has grown old, and it cannot be rejuvenated, but only recognized, by the grey in grey of philosophy; the owl of Minerva begins its flight only with the onset of dusk.[28]

Yet Hegel seemed ambivalent on this point, perhaps because clarity could have gotten him in trouble with the Prussian censors. The poet and gadfly Heinrich Heine, who claimed, without justification, to have been Hegel's favorite student, told this story:

> I often used to see him looking around anxiously as if in fear he might be understood. He was very fond of me, for he was sure I would never betray him. As a matter of fact, I then thought that he was very obsequious. Once when I grew impatient with him for saying: "All that is, is rational," he smiled strangely and remarked, "It may also be said that all that is rational must be." Then he looked about him hastily.[29]

This may be apocryphal, or it may be Heine's passing off somebody else's recollection as his own. With Heine you can never tell. But it rings true.

The anecdote poses the problem in a nutshell. Was everything the way it was supposed to be, and this the best of all possible worlds? Or was everything a product of the Absolute's struggle to realize itself, so that we lived in a state of permanent revolution? This was one of the primary tensions that shattered the Hegelian community in the years after the Master's death in 1831. The German philosophical community split into Right and Left Hegelians, who argued endlessly with each other about what Hegel had meant and where his ideas might need to be amended, corrected, or rejected.

It is fortunately not necessary to wade into that often shambolic history. As far as Wagner is concerned the essential figure was Ludwig Feuerbach, who had a better claim than Heine to the title of Hegel's favorite student. Wagner dedicated *The Artwork of the Future* to him, choosing a title that evoked the "Philosophy of the Future" that Feuerbach promised but ultimately failed to deliver.

---

28 G. W. F. Hegel, *Elements of the Philosophy of Right*, trans. Nisbet (Cambridge: Cambridge University Press, 1991), 23.
29 Heinrich Heine, "Am I a Destroyer of Faith?" (1855), in *The Poetry and Prose of Heinrich Heine*, trans. Ewen (New York: Citadel Press, 1948), 502–3.

His first acquaintance with Feuerbach was with the 1830 text *Thoughts on Death and Immortality*. This work is often ignored today, but Wagner recommended it to his friends, and its arguments have many echoes in his prose works and music dramas. It is strongly idealist and it is also surprisingly Fichtean in some ways. Feuerbach's reaction to his former teacher returned him to the gulf that Hegel had tried to overcome, the gap between conscious experience and an unknowable but active, creative reality.

For the young Feuerbach God as "Spirit" was the only reality, and in bringing ourselves to self-consciousness we had separated ourselves from that, to no good end: "By the fact that you affirm that you have an essence, you create a separation and distinction in yourself, and you express, in this separation, that you are not your own essence."[30] That separation ends with death, which returns our purportedly individual lives to the totality of "nature, soul, essence." This is not extinction but "just the withdrawal and departure of your objectivity from your subjectivity, which is eternally living activity and therefore everlasting and immortal."[31] It is not a tragedy, either, because death ratifies what we truly are, and we are never truly apart from God himself:

> Your present reflective and conscious submersion in God is but a renewal of and return to your eternal submersion, is but a bringing to awareness, a disclosure, of your original, substantial, unconscious, involuntary submersion in him.[32]

But death was not the only release from our self-created isolation. Love can open us to what we are outside of the self-aware self, especially sexual love—a thought which would become one of Wagner's favorite themes. Feuerbach wrote:

> [Y]ou love not with your personhood or as person, but only in and with essence, which is being-together, but not being-distinct or being-for-oneself. You love only because you are deeper and more than a person. ... As the human who has experienced love has experienced everything, so the human who has known love knows everything.[33] ...

---

30 Ludwig Feuerbach, *Thoughts on Death and Immortality*, trans. Massey (Berkeley: University of California Press, 1980), 107.
31 Feuerbach, *Thoughts on Death and Immortality*, 111.
32 Feuerbach, *Thoughts on Death and Immortality*, 111.
33 Feuerbach, *Thoughts on Death and Immortality*, 29–30.

In and before the object of love ... everything that is distinct and separated from it, which otherwise would be something for you, becomes nothing. All multiplicity and variety are destroyed in you as love arises in you; its arising is the disappearing of all particular existence. When you love, ... you no longer exist in your particular interests, in your affairs, in the many objects in which you used to exist. You exist now only in the one being that is object of your love. ... The solid and secure ground on which you used to stand has been pulled out from under you; you stand at the edge of total destruction; you have sunk into a bottomless abyss.[34] ...

But at the same time this perishing is a new and more excellent state of being. Accordingly, you exist and do not exist in love; love is being and not-being in one, life and death as one life. Love gives life and takes it away, destroys and engenders life.[35]

These passages could almost stand as epigraphs to *Tristan und Isolde*.

Thoughts on Death and Immortality is a rich if chaotic text, but Feuerbach was soon to repudiate its pantheist spirituality, and it was all but forgotten in the enthusiasm that greeted his *Essence of Christianity* in 1841. We all became Feuerbachians, said Engels, and none other than George Eliot translated the book into English. This excitement is hard to comprehend today, because it showed Feuerbach to be something of a one-trick pony. God is a human creation, he argued, and everything we say of him is actually an insight into what we are as a species. The "proper humanity of man" consists of "Reason, Will, [and] Affection."[36] God, therefore, is imagined to be all-wise, all-powerful, and all-loving. Feuerbach urged his readers to stop worshiping themselves in that imaginary divinity and turn instead to living by those virtues. This simple point is elaborated and reinforced through more than three hundred pages.

Feuerbach had now embraced materialism. He no longer invoked God, spirit, or some essence that pervaded and united everything, and he also left behind many of the complexities of his earlier idealism. Experience was self-explanatory, and human reason did not shape it. Instead of our separation from spirit it was the body alone that was "the basis, the subject of personality."[37] He maintained the importance of an "I-Thou" relationship, influencing Martin Buber, among others, but the

---

34 Feuerbach, *Thoughts on Death and Immortality*, 37.
35 Feuerbach, *Thoughts on Death and Immortality*, 38.
36 Ludwig Feuerbach, *The Essence of Christianity*, trans. Eliot (New York: Harper & Row, 1957), 3.
37 Feuerbach, *The Essence of Christianity*, 91.

"species being" of humanity was a mere alliance of mutually respecting individuals, coming together in a kind of division of ethical labor. "My fellow-man is my objective conscience; he makes my failings a reproach to me ... My sin is made to shrink within its limits ... by the fact that it is only mine, and not that of my fellows."[38] Even sexual love lost its cosmic significance, as it now only reinforced the independence of the partners: "the distinction between *I* and *Thou*, the fundamental condition of all personality, of all consciousness, is only real, living, ardent, when felt as the distinction between man and woman."[39]

No doubt all this came as a refreshing dose of clear-headedness in its day, but what is obvious now is that Feuerbach had very little to say aside from his one big thought. Even at that time, though, critical readers had noticed that there was little room for any kind of direction or movement in his new theory. Feuerbach had never embraced Fichte's and Hegel's idea of shared agency, and when he turned away from idealism all he could envision was a world of individuals who worked together, made advances in science and technology, established just and law-governed states, and were able to love freely and fully. That ideal, though, was static. It had no connection to any larger scheme of things or any logic of history. His later works, like the *Principles of the Philosophy of the Future*, tried to address his tendency to individualism, but they still showed readers a pretty picture, no more, and besides converting to Feuerbachian materialism they were very cloudy about how we might get there from here. In any case, Feuerbach's fifteen minutes of fame had come to an end. In the 1848 revolutions he was elected to the Frankfurt assembly that was supposed to frame a new legal and social order for Germany. He did nothing. The whole process was alien to him.

Marx saw this weakness as early as 1845, making notes that Engels, years later, would title "Theses on Feuerbach." In the first of these he complained that "all hitherto-existing materialism—that of Feuerbach included" took it for granted that objects were simply given, when it should be considering them "as human sensuous activity, practice ... Hence it happened that the active side ... was developed by idealism."[40] (This could easily be a reference to Fichte.) And his critique was not limited to Feuerbach's fundamentally static picture. It extended to the atomized individualism that Feuerbach also seemed to take for granted, as the

---

38 Feuerbach, *The Essence of Christianity*, 158, 159.
39 Feuerbach, *The Essence of Christianity*, 92.
40 https://www.marxists.org/archive/marx/works/1845/theses/index.htm.

ninth of Marx's theses shows: "The highest point reached by contemplative materialism ... is the contemplation of single individuals and of civil society."[41] On both scores he might as well have been contrasting the materialist Feuerbach with the idealist one.

What Marx wanted, and what he would spend the rest of his life developing, was an activist materialism. He had no interest in Spirit or the rationality of Fichte, the Jena Romantics, or Hegel, but he did not want to toss out their vision of an all-encompassing, creative movement made real through common agency and transpersonal solidarity, and he found a materialist grounding for such a vision in humanity's productive engagement with nature. Surprisingly, Wagner had very much the same concerns. It is not surprising, though, that he ended up closer to the idealists than he would ever be to Marx.

---

41 https://www.marxists.org/archive/marx/works/1845/theses/index.htm.

3: Wagner as Philosopher

WAGNER SEEMS TO have had, at best, an ambivalent attitude towards philosophy. His autobiography is not always a reliable source, and there are reasons to doubt his memory of his first encounter with Feuerbach, but it still provides an illuminating account of his early interest in the subject:

> I had always had an inclination to fathom the depths of philosophy, just as I had been led by the mystic influence of Beethoven's Ninth Symphony to search the deepest recesses of music. My first efforts at satisfying this longing had failed. ... I had procured Schelling's work, *Transcendental Idealism*, ... but it was in vain that I racked my brains to try and make something out of the first pages, and I always returned to my Ninth Symphony.
>
> During the latter part of my stay in Dresden I ... chose Hegel's *Philosophy of History*. A good deal of this impressed me deeply, and it now seemed as if I should ultimately penetrate into the Holy of Holies along this path. The more incomprehensible many of his speculative conclusions appeared, the more I felt myself desirous of probing the question of the "Absolute" and everything connected therewith to the core. For I so admired Hegel's powerful mind that it seemed to me he was the very keystone of all philosophical thought.
>
> The revolution intervened; the practical tendencies of a social reconstruction distracted my attention, [until] a German Catholic priest and political agitator ... drew my attention to "the only real philosopher of modern times," Ludwig Feuerbach. My new Zürich friend, the piano teacher, Wilhelm Baumgartner, made me a present of Feuerbach's book on *Tod und Unsterblichkeit* ("Death and Immortality"). The well-known and stirring lyrical style of the author greatly fascinated me as a layman. ... The frankness with which Feuerbach explains his views on these interesting questions, in the more mature parts of his book, pleased me as much by their tragic as by their social-radical tendencies. ... It was more difficult to sustain any interest in *Das Wesen des Christenthums* ("The Essence of Christianity") by the same author, for it was impossible whilst reading this work not to become conscious, however involuntarily, of the prolix and unskillful manner in which he dilates on the simple and fundamental idea, namely, religion explained from a purely subjective and psychological point of view. Nevertheless, from that

day onward I always regarded Feuerbach as the ideal exponent of the radical release of the individual from the thralldom of accepted notions, founded on the belief in authority.[1]

In the end, however, he concluded that "what had really induced [him] to attach so much importance to Feuerbach was the conclusion ... that the best philosophy was to have no philosophy ... and secondly, that only that was real which could be ascertained by the senses."[2]

Wagner was never as modest as he claimed to be. He did start off a long and important letter to Röckel, dated January 25, 1854, by restricting the Real, or true Being, to that "which is appreciable to the senses," but this common-sense realism soon disappears. Later in the same letter he redefines it in terms that echo—consciously or not—Fichte's "one life:"

> [T]he essence of reality consists of infinite multiplicity ... [an] inexhaustible multiplicity, incessantly renewed and renewing. ... [which] can only be apprehended by feeling, as the one ever-present though ever-varying element. This variability is the essence of the *real*.[3]

In no way is this a random agglomeration of disconnected events. There is only one reality, an "ever self-renewing and self-creating, ... ever self-fulfilling, self-satisfying principle," characterized by "endless cohesion."[4] All things arise within that single but ungraspably complex process.

This is a genuinely philosophical starting point, positing a kind of transcendental ground for the realm of experience, and Wagner frequently restated it or implied it even after he discovered Schopenhauer. It owes much to the biological theories of Wagner's day, and he often works it out in biological terms, but it evokes the same kind of activity that the idealists had seen in the self-manifestation of the divine or the self-realization of the Absolute. Since those thinkers had generally rejected a personal deity and all notions of providence, Wagner's focus on activity alone kept him surprisingly close to their standpoint. What counted for both was the continuous process of creation, transformation, and destruction, the endless fertility that we associate with the natural world but which underlies and forms our own lives and thoughts as well. In Wagner's words, "Nature creates and shapes unintentionally and involuntarily as the need

---

1   *My Life*, 520–22.
2   *My Life*, 522.
3   *Letters to August Roeckel*, 78, 81, 82 (January 25–26, 1854), *SL* 102.
4   *The Artwork of the Future*, 18, *PW* I, 79.

arises—out of necessity therefore—and it is this same necessity which is the creative, shaping force behind human life."[5]

Things are not so simple for conscious beings like ourselves, however. On this subject, too, Wagner revised and naturalized elements of idealism while preserving its underlying structure. To become self-conscious we had to remove ourselves from the underlying activity of all things: "The moment we humans became aware of our difference from nature, ... when we set ourselves apart from nature and ... thought began to develop within us—this was the moment we went astray, error as the first expression of consciousness." We separated ourselves from reality, and from that moment on we have tried to bridge that gap, through our personal lives, our art, our politics, and most of all through our science, philosophy, and religion; "the history of the birth of knowledge out of error is the history of the human species from primitive myth to the present day."[6]

Wagner was confident that through that struggle "enlightened nature will herself become self-aware."[7] But this would bring us to a very different kind of knowledge from the facts and theories that we usually rely on. Discovering it is difficult, and searching for it is all too likely to lead us into deeper errors than the ones we are trying to undo, bedazzling us with "fanciful image[s] based not on nature but on arbitrary willfulness."[8] We want to know, and to know that we know, but all thought is marked by the separation on which self-consciousness depends. What is real is prior to and beyond that split, so it cannot be an object of knowledge. By thinking about it we just push ourselves farther and farther away from what we think we are understanding. We mistake image for reality:

> [Humanity] has recourse to endless expedients in order to grasp the Universe as a *whole*: these expedients in all their endless complexity are simply a group of concepts; and in our pride at having thus attained to a concept of the world in its entirety, we lose sight of our true position, forgetting that after all we have grasped nothing but the concept, and that consequently we are simply taking pleasure in the instrument of our own making, while all the time we remain further removed than ever from the *reality* of the world.[9]

---

5   *The Artwork of the Future*, 13, *PW* I, 69–70.
6   All quoted text *The Artwork of the Future*, 13, *PW* I, 69–70.
7   *The Artwork of the Future*, 13, *PW* I, 69–70.
8   *The Artwork of the Future*, 14, *PW* I, 71.
9   *Letters to August Roeckel*, 80–81 (January 25–26, 1854), *SL* 302. The inaccessibility of the real ground of existence is something of a Romantic commonplace; as Tieck wrote late in life: "Is it not more devout, more noble and upstanding, to simply acknowledge that we cannot perceive this [connection],

One can read this as an anticipation of some modern philosophies of science, but Wagner first thought of it as a critique of religion: "we suppressed [nature's] physical forms in favor of a cause that is inaccessible to the senses ... conceiving the infinite cohesion of her unconscious, unintentional processes as the deliberate expression of some inchoate, finite will."[10]

It is worth pausing here. In *The Essence of Christianity* Feuerbach had more or less taken it for granted that people projected human qualities onto the divine. He had assumed this to be the result of a primitive animism; in the distant past we didn't know enough about why the sun rose and set, why there was death, why there were storms and earthquakes and so on, so we made up gods to explain these facts. Wagner had a much more sophisticated starting point; he could explain why there was a place for the gods to begin with. They (or He) occupied a throne that we had set up ourselves.

Consciousness begins with a fall. Once we had separated ourselves from reality we could no longer simply live in it. It had become a puzzle that we had to solve. Everything, both good and bad, seemed to have its own life and follow its own rules, and once we started thinking of ourselves as outside observers we had figure out those rules and "grasp the Universe as a *whole*." We wanted to explain things and events that seemed to stand in front of us, and that led us to imagine that these were put together and managed by something that stood behind them, a figure we could imagine only on the model of our own isolated, active, and thinking selves: a god, in other words. As Wagner wrote in *Opera and Drama*, "*the concordant action* of human and natural forces in general ... appears super-human and supernatural by the very fact that it is ascribed to *one* imagined individual, represented in the shape of Man."[11]

Wagner came to see, too, that these intellectual and emotional needs are at work in more than just religious life. This was a step beyond Feuerbach. We can get rid of the gods, Wagner understood, but it is much harder to stop asking the kinds of questions that those gods were designed to answer, and this is why science was as limited as religion. He insisted

---

that our knowledge can only relate to the individual, and that we must resign [to any further claim]?" (Quoted in Manfred Frank, trans. Millán, *The Philosophical Foundations of Early German Romanticism* (Albany: SUNY Press, 2003), 212.

10   *The Artwork of the Future*, 13, *PW* I, 70. Cooke sees superstition as the "original" error. Deryck Cooke, *I Saw the World End* (Oxford: Oxford University Press, 1979), 254. Wagner's text, however, identifies the separation of humanity from nature as the primordial error of consciousness; the positing of a cause behind nature is a consequence of that error, and is not identical with it.

11   Richard Wagner, *Opera and Drama*, trans. Ellis, *PW* II, 154. He cites Feuerbach in this connection.

that "at the beginning of science we stand in the same relation to life as we did when we began to set our own human life apart from nature;"[12] there may be no gods involved, but we are still trying to find an external principle that explains away the world of the senses. This is a doomed enterprise, however. Science generates just another set of limited ideas that can never capture a limitless reality. "The essence of science is therefore as finite as that of life is infinite, just as error is finite while truth is infinite."[13]

We cannot think our way out of those constraints. Understanding that impasse leads some of us to reject the "barren illusion" of theory, "to turn to *reality* and to approach it by means of feeling." But "how is this to be done, seeing that *reality* as an imagined *whole* can only be made intelligible to the intellect, and cannot be brought into relation with feeling?"[14]

Wagner's uncle Adolf had suggested to Tieck that idealism was a "hunger cure" that removed us from the purely human so we could recuperate in a world of both nature and humanity.[15] Wagner himself had a different "hunger cure." It was giving up the fiction of a world that could be grasped by the mind. We do not need right views or better theories; "we must entirely renounce the pursuit of the Universal."[16] What we need is the most radical kind of trust. Much as Fichte did, Wagner insisted that we could embrace reality only by surrendering the Ego of self-consciousness and the detached thinking that self-consciousness makes possible.

Wagner asked Röckel: "To be real—to live—what is it but to be born, to grow, to bloom, to wither and to die?"[17] He went on:

> Therefore to be at one with truth is to give oneself up as a sentient human being wholly and entirely to reality—to encounter birth, growth, bloom, blight and decay frankly, with joy and with sorrow, and to live to the full this life made up of happiness and suffering— so to live and so to die.[18]

---

12   *The Artwork of the Future*, 14, *PW* I, 72.
13   *The Artwork of the Future*, 14, *PW* I, 72.
14   *Letters to August Roeckel*, 81 (January 25–26, 1854), *SL* 302, translation altered.
15   *Letters to and from Ludwig Tieck and His Circle: Unpublished Letters from the Period of German Romanticism Including the Unpublished Correspondence of Sophie and Ludwig Tieck*, ed. Percy Matenko, Edwin H. Zeydel, and Bertha M. Masche (Chapel Hill: University of North Carolina Press, 1967), 164, translation mine.
16   *Letters to August Roeckel*, 82 (January 25–26, 1854), *SL* 303.
17   *Letters to August Roeckel*, 81–82 (January 25–26, 1854), *SL* 302–3.
18   *Letters to August Roeckel*, 82 (January 25–26, 1854), *SL* 302–3.

It is probably not a coincidence that Wagner was, at least briefly, very taken with the Sufi poet Hafiz, whom he praised to Röckel as "the greatest of all poets."[19] It is also tempting to see this as an anticipation of Nietzsche's *amor fati,* the deep sense "that one wants nothing to be different, not forward, not backward, not in all eternity. Not merely bear what is necessary, still less conceal it ... but *love* it."[20]

For it was love, and sexual love in particular, that Wagner saw as the path towards selfless oneness with the Real. He told Röckel that "we can only fully grasp a phenomenon if we can at one and the same time completely absorb it, and be absorbed by it," and to achieve that absorption, he added, "We must look to love, and to love only":[21]

> [O]nly that which is real can be eternal, and it is through love that we attain to the most perfect manifestation of reality; therefore Love only is eternal. The fact is, egoism ceases at the moment when the "I" passes into the "Thou."[22]

We believe that we are separate beings who must armor ourselves against an indifferent or hostile world, and our finitude "has power to strike terror into our souls; but it can do so only if we have lost our hold on *reality*. If, on the contrary, we are possessed by a sense of the reality of love, that terror vanishes, for love annihilates the notion of limitation."[23] At that point we let go of the ego and of all the hedges and defenses with which we struggle to protect it. There is only the real, and in love we sense and embrace our identity with its movement. That is why falling in love seems like a deeper wisdom than anything we can think or speak, and why every step that lovers take can feel effortlessly choreographed.

Wagner wrote endlessly about love in all of its forms, at least those that he could accept within his at-least-publicly heteronormative outlook.[24] But it is essential to recognize that he did not give it such importance because it made people nice or kind. It was not worthy because it inspired us to do good deeds or to treat others as they deserved to be treated. Love was important because "it is through love that we attain to

---

19 *Letters to August Roeckel,* 59 (September 12, 1852), *SL* 270.
20 Friedrich Nietzsche, "Ecce Homo," in *Basic Writings of Nietzsche,* 714.
21 *Letters to August Roeckel,* 82–83 (January 25–26, 1854), *SL* 303.
22 *Letters to August Roeckel,* 86, *SL* 304.
23 *Letters to August Roeckel,* 86, *SL* 304.
24 He praised Spartan homosexual love but this was premised on a belief that "it excluded the motive of physical, selfish pleasure." *The Artwork of the Future,* 63–64, *PW* I, 168.

the most perfect manifestation of reality."[25] We therefore misunderstand much of the *Ring* if we think of this as a desirable or socially beneficial emotional state or as "a natural instinctive need for mutual love and fellowship," in Deryck Cooke's words.[26] Love is central to human life because of its transformative and even destructive power. It returns us to reality, and so long as we live in love we are freed from the misleading separation on which we had premised our conscious lives.

Love has both power and inestimable value because it aligns us with the all-encompassing activity of what is real, the ever-flowing river in which we gladly immerse ourselves. It is a liberating force, freeing us from the selfish compulsion to look after our own private needs and impulses, and through it we live as willing participants in the life we share with all others. Like Fichte's ethical person, we become pure presentations of reality, and this—not self-indulgence or untrammeled power—is genuine freedom. Wagner never developed a theory of ethics, but ethical concerns are rarely absent when he talks about love, and one can easily trace a line that goes from Kant's moral law through Fichte's egoless morality to Wagner's praise of love.

Erotic union, for Wagner, was both immersion in reality and a passage into shared agency. "Now, a human being is both *man* and *woman*, and it is only when these two are united that the real human being exists, and thus it is only by love that man and woman attain to the full measure of humanity. But when nowadays we talk of a human being, such heartless blockheads are we that quite involuntarily we only think of man."[27] And that union is a model for all truly human connections. "Every other manifestation of love can be traced back to that one absorbingly real feeling,"[28] and it therefore grounds the community of the entire human race. People "only find understanding, redemption and satisfaction in a higher element; and this higher element is the human species. ... And the individual human can only satisfy his or her need for love by giving, indeed by giving him or herself to others and at the highest level to humankind."[29] Just as in sexual love, this is not self-denial but self-realization: "only by wholly

---

25 *Letters to August Roeckel*, 86 (January 25–26, 1854), *SL* 304 (Note that Wagner's text does not refer to the "sentiment" of love, as the *SL* translation has it).

26 Cooke repeats this formula almost verbatim in many passages starting around p. 253 of *I Saw the World End*.

27 *Letters to August Roeckel*, 84 (January 25–26, 1854), *SL* 303. The *Symposium* was a favorite of Wagner's, and he may well be echoing the fable that Plato ascribes to Aristophanes.

28 *Letters to August Roeckel*, 83 (January 25–26, 1854), *SL* 303.

29 *The Artwork of the Future*, 27, *PW* I, 96–97.

merging with the other, with the community therefore, that you can be fully what you are, what you can be and what you reasonably want to be. Only in communism is egoism fully satisfied."[30]

This underpins Wagner's utopian politics, but for him it also led to art. In the early 1850s he had little use for religion, which he saw as just another "external, imaginary power" whose votaries concocted images which they sold to us as pictures of the real. They were nothing like that, of course, so it was left to art to accomplish what religion only claimed to do. Art would show humanity that it reflects and embodies "the inner necessity of nature." It would bring reality to light. That gives it a quasi-religious, even sacramental function.[31]

For Wagner art is a form of revelation; it is nature itself that gives it birth. In the very first sentence of *The Artwork of the Future* he hints at this in a statement too compressed to be taken in quickly: "Humans are to nature as art is to humans." He goes on to expand this thought:

> Once nature had developed the right conditions for humans to exist then humans came spontaneously into being: as soon as human life develops the conditions for art to emerge, so art springs spontaneously to life.[32]

These are separate moments in the same activity. One and the same movement fashions both human consciousness and art, and in both thinking and artistic creativity an invisible reality is made visible. Just as nature becomes aware of itself through humanity, humanity becomes aware of itself through art.

If Wagner had read through Schelling's *System of Transcendental Idealism*, or if he had flipped to the end after "racking his brains to make sense of its first pages," he would have seen that, for Schelling, all philosophy culminated in the work of art, which "reflects to us the identity of the conscious and unconscious activities."[33] "To put it more briefly," Schelling had written, "nature begins as unconscious and ends as conscious," and through art "the unconscious activity operates as it were through the conscious, to the point of attaining complete identity therewith."[34]

---

30   *The Artwork of the Future*, 28, PW I, 99.
31   *The Artwork of the Future*, 14–15, PW I, 71.
32   *The Artwork of the Future*, 13, PW I, 69.
33   Friedrich Schelling, *System of Transcendental Idealism*, trans. Heath (Charlottesville: University of Virginia Press, 1978), 225. As was typical of Schelling, he soon gave up on this idea.
34   Schelling, *System of Transcendental Idealism*, 219.

This would be quite easy to translate into Wagner's terms, but doing that would miss the point. Schelling saw this entire process as a private one, carried out by individuals and ultimately by the solitary Romantic genius, who alone could unite the infinite productivity of nature with an infinite freedom of thought.[35] Nothing could be less Wagnerian. Wagner did generally feel himself to be solitary, but he saw that as the fault of his times, not as the precondition for art; the "artist of the future" would be "necessarily the community of all artists."[36] As a man of the theater, especially, he insisted that artistic work was always collaborative, and the camaraderie of the artists and artisans at Bayreuth was a delight to him; "Very often the relations between Wagner and his artists were extremely jolly and free-and-easy. At the last rehearsal in the salon of the Hotel Sommer he actually, out of sheer high spirits, stood on his head."[37] He dismissed talk of artistic genius as a gift or an "absolute windfall" (think of the play and movie *Amadeus*) as "uncommonly vapid and superficial."[38]

Real genius was different. It was nothing but "receptive force" applied to something that had already fashioned itself within the life of the community:

> That which operates so mightily upon this [receptive] force that it must finally come forth to full productiveness, we have in truth to regard as the real fashioner and former, as the only furthering condition for that force's efficacy, and this is the Art already evolved outside that separate force, the Art which from the artworks of the ancient and the modern world has shaped itself into a universal Substance, and hand in hand with actual Life, reacts upon the individual with the character of the force that I have elsewhere named the *communistic*.[39]

"Thus the poet cannot create, but only the folk; or the poet only in so far as he comprehends and utters, represents, the creation of the folk."[40] Art is thus profoundly social. Wagner saw this ideal at work in ancient Greece, and especially in Athenian tragedy, which he read closely and creatively, if sometimes oddly. His term for the unconscious artwork of the community was "Mythos," and in Mythos "all the shaping impulse of the Folk" collaborated in showing to "its senses a broadest grouping of

---

35 Schelling, *System of Transcendental Idealism*, 228.
36 *The Artwork of the Future*, 78, *PW* I, 196.
37 Quoted in Mann, "Sufferings and Greatness of Richard Wagner," 329.
38 Richard Wagner, *A Communication to My Friends*, trans. Ellis, *PW* I, 288.
39 *A Communication to My Friends*, *PW* I, 288.
40 Richard Wagner, "Sketches (1849–1851)," trans. Ellis, *PW* VIII, 349.

the most manifold phenomena, and in the most succinct of shapes."[41] What the tragedian did was make the Mythos visible; "the shapes that had been in Mythos merely shapes of Thought, were now presented in actual bodily portrayal by living men: so the actually represented Action now compressed itself, in thorough keeping with the mythic essence, into a compact, plastic whole."[42]

Putting it briefly, "Tragedy is nothing other than the artistic completion of the Myth itself; while the Myth is the poem of a life-view in common."[43] This social grounding is what makes it possible for art to be "the faithful, conscious image of the authentic human being and of a human life lived according to natural necessity."[44] The calling of art is to make that necessity, that activity, into something sensible and therefore knowable, thus completing a kind of circle: in self-consciousness the unity of nature splinters into sensible events, which are woven together by the community in its stories and images, and through art these elements are focused and fused into sensible representations that show us our original identity with reality itself. Art is the mirror that shows us that we ourselves are the mirror of nature.

This is not a primal unity, as Nattiez thinks.[45] It is something achieved, and we can see the *Ring* cycle as an attempt to achieve just that. But this is also why Wagner's tetralogy is such a monster. It has something alien about it. Looking around him Wagner saw nothing like the idealized collective life he thought he could see in ancient Athens. It was exactly the opposite, an "anti-art way of life."[46] Thinking had cut itself off from "the totality of all reality," seeing itself "not as the last and most contingent, but rather as the first and least contingent agency, and therefore as the foundation and cause of nature," and once that happened "the bond of necessity snap[ped] and arbitrary wilfulness rage[d] unchecked ... through the workings of thought, unleashing a tide of madness into the real world."[47]

Genuine art begins with "the real, physical human presence, from his life need, whose pre-condition in turn is nature's actual, tangible presence." In a community shaped by the give-and-take of free people art was conservative. It made manifest what the people themselves had

---

41 *Opera and Drama, PW* II, 154.
42 *Opera and Drama, PW* II, 154.
43 *Opera and Drama, PW* II, 156.
44 *The Artwork of the Future*, 14, *PW* I, 71.
45 Nattiez, *Wagner Androgyne*, 18.
46 *The Artwork of the Future*, 20, *PW* I, 82.
47 *The Artwork of the Future*, 20, *PW* I, 32.

felt and done, as they lived close to the roots of experience and thus to the necessity of the real. (This is more emotional openness than some back-to-nature primitivism.) In a world of "nature-sundered" individuals, though, the circle through which reality comes to self-awareness is broken, and concepts and ideas about things replace the things themselves. Wagner calls the source of those ideas *Geist,* an untranslatable word meaning mind or spirit, and its triumph, unmoored from natural necessity and the real lives of a human community, is the exact opposite of the human freedom it might seem to exalt. It makes real human beings interchangeable and expendable:

> If the spirit created nature, if thought made reality, if the philosopher precedes the human then nature, reality and human beings are no longer necessary, their existence is superfluous, harmful even ... Then nature, reality and human beings only gain meaning, their existence is only justified when the spirit—that unconditional spirit, which is cause, effect and law unto itself—uses them according to its own absolute, sovereign pleasure. If the spirit in itself is necessity then it is life that is arbitrary, a fantastic masquerade, an idle distraction, a frivolous whim, [and] every purely human need is a luxury, [while] luxury on the other hand is a need.[48]

Real life vanishes from view. Since we are never apart from reality, though, the belief that we can stand above it and dictate our terms to it can only be a delusion, and any cultural product that proceeds from a delusion can only be sterile. We produce dead imitations of real art, following fashion rather than necessity:

> Fashion ... requires nature's absolute obedience; it demands the complete self-denial of true need in favor of an imaginary one; it forces humans' natural sense of beauty into the worship of ugliness; it kills our health to teach us to love sickness; it destroys our strength and power to make us find contentment in our weakness. Where the most laughable fashion reigns, there nature is seen to be most ridiculous; where the most criminally unnatural reigns, there the expression of nature appears the highest crime; where insanity takes the place of truth, there truth must be locked in the insane asylum.[49]

---

48 *The Artwork of the Future,* 20, *PW* I, 83. (Includes quotations in previous paragraph.) Wagner's *Geist* should not be confused with Hegel's *Geist,* which is closer to Wagner's unknowable real.
49 *The Artwork of the Future,* 20–21, *PW* I, 84.

And Wagner could see no way out: "the needs of art can never exist where fashion dictates the rules by which we live."[50]

Under these conditions art could not be conservative. "With us," he wrote in *Art and Revolution*, "true Art is *revolutionary*, because its very existence is opposed to the ruling spirit of the community."[51] In that same essay, though, he admitted that the social conditions for true art were missing. "The perfect Art-work, the great united utterance of a free and lovely public life, the *Drama, Tragedy* ... is not yet born again: ... Only the great Revolution of Mankind ... can win for us this Art-work."[52]

He was sure that this "great Revolution" would come soon. Though the culture of the present day had set itself against nature, its "heavy load ... will one day grow so ponderous" that "down-trod, never-dying Nature" will "hurl the whole cramping burden from her, with one sole thrust."[53] "Nature and her fulness" would then be the wealth of the whole human community, equally, and the needs which had blighted the lives of the poor would be cast away (onto machines, apparently); "then will man's whole enfranchised energy proclaim itself as naught but pure *artistic* impulse."[54] Art would be reborn.

But Wagner did not want to wait, and he was more inconsistent than usual on this point: "The true artist who has already grasped the proper standpoint," he maintained, "may labour even now—for this standpoint is present with us—upon the Art-work of the Future!"[55] He would turn back to a Mythos from the distant past, reconstructed through his own prodigious if undisciplined reading. He claimed the right to do this because, he said, "The incomparable thing about the Mythos is, that it is true for all time."[56] Yet the *Ring* had no place in the life of its own day. In the early 1850s, with the idea of Bayreuth some years in the future, Wagner was convinced that it could be performed only after a revolution, not those that had failed or been put down in 1848 and 1849 but the grander one he expected, because only "the men of the Revolution" would understand that it made clear "the *meaning* of that Revolution,

---

50 *The Artwork of the Future*, 21, *PW* I, 85.
51 Richard Wagner, *Art and Revolution*, trans. Ellis, *PW* I, 51–52.
52 *Art and Revolution*, *PW* I, 53.
53 *Art and Revolution*, *PW* I, 55.
54 *Art and Revolution*, *PW* I, 57. Oscar Wilde's "The Soul of Man Under Socialism" is a witty elaboration of this idea.
55 *Art and Revolution*, *PW* I, 60–61.
56 *Opera and Drama*, *PW* II, 191.

in its noblest sense."⁵⁷ And after that would come the truly revolutionary art, one that would bring about "the ascension of the *egoistic* essence of the individual into the *communistic* essence of the human race; the concretion of the abstract idea of Man into the actual, true and blissful common-being of *Mankind*."⁵⁸

---

57 To Theodor Uhlig, November 12, 1851, *SL* 234.
58 Richard Wagner, "Art and Climate," trans. Ellis, *PW* I, 261.

4: The Future that Failed

THESE ARE DANGEROUS ideas, and not always in a good way. Karol Berger sees them pointing towards a terrifying post-political future, arguing that "[i]t is the central paradox of *Götterdämmerung*, and hence of the *Ring*, that it demonstrates the hopelessly utopian nature of the anarchist ideal that it promotes."[1] He assumes the primacy of "naturally isolated and egoistic individuals"[2] and insists that Wagner's ideal is a community of sovereign individuals "held together by spontaneous sympathy, without any ... mediation" provided by a social contract or law. This, like Marx's early communism, must entail despotism: "the abolishing of legal limits on individual freedom cannot but lead to the domination of the strong over the weak."[3]

Berger takes it for granted that we are "naturally isolated and egoistic individuals," and he dismisses the possibility that this construction of experience could be a "contingent product of recent historical development."[4] From a global perspective, however, that is exactly what it is, and it is what Fichte, especially, had sought to deconstruct. To take it as something self-evidently true, as Berger does, is to limit the range of thinkable social and political possibilities, and that is a genuine problem. Whatever the merits of his solutions, if he is really proposing any, Wagner's philosophy and drama raise issues which cannot be so easily dismissed.

Theory aside, the man who created the character of Alberich knew how easily the unfettered will of the strong could overpower the needs of the weak. Wagner was never a radical individualist in the Max Stirner or Silicon Valley billionaire mode, and his imagined free community was made up of those who could divest themselves of the drive to separation

---

1   Karol Berger, *Beyond Reason: Wagner contra Nietzsche* (Berkeley: University of California Press, 2017), 155. Bernard Williams's more nuanced analysis, in "Wagner and the Transcendence of Politics," sees the suggestion of "a higher, transcendental politics, of a peculiarly threatening kind" as at least in part a product of the *Ring*'s historical situation and the power of its musical rhetoric. Bernard Williams, *On Opera* (New Haven, CT: Yale University Press, 2006), 87.
2   Berger, *Beyond Reason*, 185.
3   Berger, *Beyond Reason*, 185–86.
4   Berger, *Beyond Reason*, 185.

and domination. Moreover, while his concrete political ideas, even at their best, were often treacherously naïve, Wagner recognized most of the time that mediating social institutions are essential to the flourishing of any human community. He saw classical Greek culture, which of course had its own political institutions, as grounded in a continual conversation of word and deed through which ideas of humanity and human relations were generated and expressed as myth, and on formal social rituals such as the theater festivals though which those communal ideas were refined and presented as models or warnings. He was fully aware of the injustices on which this social system rested, too; as he wrote in *Art and Revolution*:

> The Slave, by sheer reason of the assumed necessity of his slavery, has exposed the null and fleeting nature of all the strength and beauty of exclusive Grecian manhood, and has shown to all time that Beauty and Strength, as attributes of public life, can then alone prove lasting blessings, when they are the common gifts of all mankind.[5]

This "sin of history" against the human nature of the slave class was visited on the slave-owners themselves, who "soon found out that—when all men cannot be free alike and happy—all men must suffer alike as slaves."[6] Wagner's social egalitarianism is rooted in this insight.

What Wagner was reaching for was not a post-political future, as Berger claims, but a post-individualist politics, and the fact that the latter is all but impossible to formulate does not mean that it is a utopian fantasy or that these two are one and the same. He knew what was necessary, but not how this was to be accomplished. That does not make the task any less real or any less pressing. The famous closing gesture of Chereau's centennial *Ring*, where the cast turns towards the audience, is exactly in keeping with Wagner's intentions; we are being left with a challenge, not a message. That so many interpretations ignore this and send the cosmos of the *Ring* into a fiery death only suggests the truism that it is easier to imagine the end of the world than it is to imagine the end of capitalism.

The criticisms are stronger, though, when one turns away from Burkean condemnations of post-political thinking to actual history. As is all too well known, Wagner's ideas were quickly turned into ideological cover for a nascent European far right. He himself was the first to move in that direction, attacking Jews as archetypes of nature-sundered humanity, people incapable of true creativity because they were cut off from their

---

5   *Art and Revolution*, *PW* I, 50.
6   *Art and Revolution*, *PW* I, 51. In both quotations I have omitted Ellis's italics.

roots. This was unjustifiable and not at all theoretically necessary, but it served to rationalize Wagner's irrational hatred of Jews as a whole, and after his death, thanks to the deplorable politics of the Bayreuth circle, the antisemitic views of his widow, their daughter Eva's marriage to the English racist Houston Stewart Chamberlain, and their daughter-in-law Winifred's devotion to Hitler, Wagner and his festival came to be identified first with proto-fascism and ultimately with Nazism.

Hitler may have been the sole fanatical Wagnerian among the Nazi elite, but some of Wagner's texts and imagery and selected extracts from his scores seemed to anticipate the blood-and-soil ideology of National Socialism. Yet Nazi "culture" and governance were hardly in keeping with Wagner's theories. His ideal art was a mirror, not a model, arising from the shared creativity of ordinary people, and the reality of Fascism was exactly the opposite of this. As the sterile classicism of Arno Breker, the "official state sculptor" of Nazi Germany,[7] might suggest, it was never the organic cultivation of a grounded form of communal life. It was the imposition from above of a fraudulent image of community, enforced by a regime of propagandists and policemen far more intrusive and destructive of anything worthwhile in life than individualist capitalism has ever needed. So far from realizing a Wagnerian ideal, it actively suppressed any creative spontaneity. Instead of fostering a community that could shape itself and give birth to genuine art, it tried to force an entire nation into the mold of a pseudo-artistic idea, and it channeled a murderous rage toward anyone who seemed to threaten that idea. It killed art in the name of the people and killed people in the name of art.

Actually existing fascism was deeply anti-Wagnerian. It is not always easy, though, to separate Wagner's philosophy from its distorted echoes, and his own character and prejudices make that even harder. It is worth doing all the same. Wagner's imaginative development of a kind of materialist idealism deserves to be rescued from right-wing Wagnerians. It may need to be rescued from Wagner himself.

In the late 1840s, at least, Wagner had clearly been a man of the left, committed to the most progressive of ideals, and he was still talking about revolutionary change years after that. In the early spring of 1848, after the French monarchy had been overthrown, Saxony—where Wagner lived—and other German states agreed to the creation of a National Assembly which would write a constitution for a more unified and democratic Germany. The Assembly first met in Frankfurt on May 18, 1848,

---

7   Richard Evans, *The Third Reich in Power, 1933–1939* (New York: Penguin Books, 2005), 167.

and the very next day Wagner wrote to a friend warning that it was pointless for a constitution to be drawn up "until such time as we have *cleared the ground*."[8] He was right to be worried.

Wagner was Kappellmeister of the opera house in Dresden, so he was technically in the employ of the King of Saxony, and in his first contributions to the "springtime of the peoples" he tried to strike a middle ground between crown and populace. In letters and a public address he proposed a republican monarchy, encouraging the King to ally himself with the populace and do away with aristocratic privilege and legal inequality.[9] This was not as implausible as it might sound; as Borchmeyer notes, Wagner was aligning "himself with a respectable revolutionary tradition embodied in countless writings emanating from the circle of apologists of the French Revolution."[10] He appears to have kept up these hopes into the late autumn and early winter of 1848, when he wrote a prose sketch for an operatic work on the Nibelungen myth and a poetic text for a "grand opera" to be called *Siegfrieds Tod*, "Siegfried's Death." These both end with the reaffirmation of Wotan's authority as king of the gods, and the opera was to close with a choral hymn to the deity.[11]

As proceedings in Frankfurt continued, however, Wagner's political position became more radical. His assistant August Röckel started a left-wing journal, *Die Volksblätter* (the "people's pages"), and Wagner wrote at least two incendiary articles for him at roughly the same time as the National Assembly was debating the liberal, reformist Imperial Constitution that won parliamentary approval on March 27, 1849.[12] Both of Wagner's articles demand changes far more sweeping than any constitution could bring about.

The first, "Man and Existing Society," was published on February 10, 1849. In it Wagner pronounced that "[i]n the year 1848 Man's fight against Established Society began." Maneuverings between monarchies

---

8   Letter to Franz Jacob Wigard, May 19, 1848, *SL* 139.
9   Letter to August von Lüttichau, June 18, 1848, *SL* 140–41 (von Lüttichau was Intendant at the Dresden Court Theater); Richard Wagner, "Speech to the *Vaterlandsverein*," June 14, 1848, trans. Ellis, *PW* IV, 136–44.
10 Borchmeyer, *Richard Wagner: Theory and Theatre*, 9.
11 This is discussed in detail in chapter 5, below.
12 Some doubt has been cast on their authorship, without any clear resolution of the issue, but there can be little doubt that Wagner was in sympathy with their contents; see, for example, *The Artwork of the Future*, 19, *PW* I, 81: "The people however need only to deny through the deed that which is indeed nothing... , to destroy what's worth destroying, so that the future, unveiled, stands before them of its own accord."

and factions of the ruling classes, "the old comedy of a struggle for supremacy between the various sections of Society," could not conceal the reality that these were "nothing further than the death-throes of a body from which the soul, its life, has flown already, nothing beyond the last mists of night set scudding by the rising sun."[13]

Humanity must "do with *consciousness* what the age demands." Its battle with existing society had come about, he argued, because "the ordering of established Society runs counter to the destiny, the right of Man." That right is, naturally, the realization of its destiny, which is "through the ever higher perfecting of [its] mental, moral, and corporeal faculties, to attain an ever higher, purer happiness."[14] But this cannot be accomplished by individuals; "man is of himself unable to attain his destiny[;] in himself he has no strength to unfold the innate germ that marks him from the beasts." Humanity must join together, because

> The more extended, more intimate the union, the more amply unfolds the spirit, purer becomes the morality, more many-sided wax the needs, and with them grows the strength of men to satisfy them.

Thus, "only in union can men find the force to lead them toward their destiny; but only where the force exists, can the destiny be also."[15]

Wagner had not yet worked out the relatively sophisticated dialectic of *The Artwork of the Future*, but by 1848 and 1849 he was already committed to its initial presupposition. The force that drives humanity towards its destiny, which leads it ever on towards the shining heights, is a ceaseless creativity that unfolds as natural needs and their fulfillment, uniting all: "The individual is but a fraction of the whole; isolated, he is nothing; only as a part of the whole, does he find his mission, right, his happiness."[16] What stood in the way of that process, Wagner argued at the time, was that "our Established Society" was "without knowledge, without consciousness of her task." It left everything to chance, which "decides if we shall near our destiny, attain our right, [and] be happy." This was both unfair and inefficient. The battle against existing society

---

13 Richard Wagner, "Man and Established Society," trans. Ellis, *PW* VIII, 227.

14 "Man and Established Society," *PW* VIII, 228 (all quotes up to note). I omit some of Ellis's copious italics.

15 "Man and Established Society," *PW* VIII, 229.

16 "Man and Established Society," *PW* VIII, 229–30.

was thus "the war of consciousness with chance, of mind with mindlessness, morality with evil, [and] of strength against weakness."[17]

Two months later Wagner evoked the same creative force and personified it as the unstoppable activity of Revolution, "the ever-rejuvenating mother of mankind":

> where her mighty foot steps falls in ruins what an idle whim had built for aeons, and the hem of her robe sweeps its last remains away. But in her wake there opens out a ne'er-dreamt paradise of happiness, illumed by kindly sunbeams; and where her foot had trodden down, spring fragrant flowers from the soil, and jubilant songs of freed mankind fill full the air.[18]

Revolution tells the people that she has come to break all fetters, "to redeem you from the arms of death and pour young Life through all your veins ... I, the eternal destroyer, fulfill the law and fashion ever-youthful life."[19] The order of things will be destroyed "from its root up," and

> Annulled be the fancy that gives Death power over Life, the Past o'er the Future. The law of the dead is their own law; it shares their lot and dies with them; it shall not govern Life. Life is law unto itself. And since the Law is for the living, not the dead, and ye are living, with none conceivable above you, ye yourselves are the law, your own free will the sole and highest law.[20]

Wagner was no longer thinking in terms of conscious social engineering; the revolution would set all of humanity free. His vision now had no place for a state of any kind, for none would be needed in the universal fraternity to come: "Nor hate, nor envy, grudge nor enmity, be henceforth found among you; as brothers shall ye all who live know one another, and free, free in willing, free in doing, free in enjoying, shall ye attest the worth of life."[21]

James Treadwell saw this and other aspects of Wagner's life as suggestive evidence of a "delusional insanity," writing: "There is certainly something almost comically visionary about his revolutionary ambitions of the late 1840s."[22] They may not have looked that way to Wagner's

---

17 "Man and Established Society," *PW* VIII, 230.
18 Richard Wagner, "The Revolution," trans. Ellis, *PW* VIII, 232–33.
19 "The Revolution," *PW* VIII, 235.
20 "The Revolution," *PW* VIII, 236.
21 "The Revolution," *PW* VIII, 238.
22 James Treadwell, *Interpreting Wagner* (New Haven, CT: Yale University Press, 2003), 70.

contemporaries, though. Millenarian and even apocalyptic outcomes had seemed imminent during the early years of the French Revolution,[23] and Hegel, Schelling, and/or Hölderlin's "Earliest Program" from 1796 insisted that "every state necessarily manipulates free people like machinery, and it should not do so; hence it must *cease to exist*."[24] Such visions were still associated with revolutionary change decades later. A canto of Arthur Hugh Clough's superb narrative poem *Amours de Voyage* is devoted to the suppression of the Roman Republic, which had been proclaimed on April 25, 1849, and in it Clough's antihero Claude admits that he had

> Never predicted Parisian millenniums, never beheld a
> New Jerusalem coming down dressed like a bride out of heaven
> Right on the Place de la Concorde ... [25]

When people thought about change in the 1840s their imaginations were far more vivid than ours are today.

The *Volksblätter* articles are very much of their time. They can be read as a fusion of Wagner's biologistic starting point with the anarchism of the Russian revolutionary Mikhail Bakunin, with whom Röckel and Wagner had struck up a friendship. Bakunin remains widely misunderstood; Simon Callow, in his popular biography of Wagner, described him as "the most notorious terrorist in the world, the Osama bin Laden of his day."[26] This is wildly untrue. He was happy to plan or instigate uprisings against authority, but Bakunin was never involved in terrorism of any kind, and there was always something impractical and unworldly about him. An 1848 compatriot said of him: "What a man! on the first day of the revolution he is simply a treasure; but on the second day there is no way out but to shoot him."[27] He was avidly attached to destruction, but only to clear the way for a rebuilding; Wagner recalled, "He comforted himself by saying that the creators of the new order of things would arise of themselves, but that our sole business in the meantime was to find the power to destroy" and that "in other respects [Bakunin] proved a really amiable and tender-hearted man."[28] What Bakunin expected after

---

23 See Clarke Garrett, *Respectable Folly: Millenarians and the French Revolution in France and England* (Baltimore, MD: Johns Hopkins University Press, 1975).
24 "Earliest Program for a System of German Idealism," 72.
25 Canto II, lines 18–20.
26 Simon Callow, *Being Wagner* (New York: Vintage Books, 2017), 78.
27 Quoted in Samuel Rezneck, "The Social and Political Theory of Mikhail Bakunin," *The American Political Science Review* 21, no. 2 (1927): 272, n10.
28 *My Life*, 469.

the tyranny of the state was destroyed was a bottom-up community of free people, a confederation of confederations—an anarchist vision later embraced by activists like Murray Bookchin.

This theory rested on more than some naïve faith in human goodness. Bakunin was deeply religious in his early years, and he was strongly drawn to Fichte's lectures on the blessed life, which emphasized the ultimate identity of humanity with God. That identity also guaranteed a universal harmony. "'The goal of life', Bakunin wrote in 1836, 'is God—not the God to whom men pray in the churches …, but the God who lives in mankind and is exalted with the exaltation of man.'"[29] This intoxicated spirituality carried over into his political enthusiasms; what he looked for was "a *this-worldly* realization—which flows from the divine nature, the primordial equality, and the communion of free men—of that which comprises the divine nature of Christianity."[30] Remove the religiosity and the parallels with Wagner's thoughts of the time are impossible to miss, as are the echoes of Fichte. "'Away with all religious and philosophic theories,' [Bakunin] wrote in 1845, 'the truth is not theory but activity—life itself; to know the truth is not simply to think, but to live—and life is more than thinking: life is a miraculous embodiment of truth.'"[31]

"We are on the eve of a world-wide historical turning point," wrote Bakunin,[32] but it would not be the turning point that he, Röckel, or Wagner wanted. As moderate as it was, the proposed Imperial Constitution was unacceptable to the King of Saxony. He dissolved the kingdom's parliament, and on May 3, 1849, a popular uprising broke out in response. The king and his loyalists fled Dresden and a provisional government took over.

This was no mere bourgeois revolution. It was competently organized and had surprisingly broad popular support. According to Christopher Clark, "Across Saxony as a whole, 75,000 people were enrolled in 280 radical associations," and while the majority were workers, "master artisans, journeymen and laborers," other supporters were "teachers, artists, lawyers and businessmen."[33] The architect Gottfried Semper, whose designs

---

29 V. V. Zenkovsky, *A History of Russian Philosophy*, trans. Kline (New York: Columbia University Press, 1953), 248.

30 Zenkovsky, *A History of Russian Philosophy*, 253.

31 Zenkovsky, *A History of Russian Philosophy*, 255. On the influence of Fichte on Bakunin, see Robert M. Cutler, "Bakunin's Anti-Jacobinism: 'Secret Societies' For Self-Emancipating Collectivist Social Revolution," *Anarchist Studies* 22, no. 2 (2014): 22.

32 Zenkovsky, *A History of Russian Philosophy*, 255.

33 Christopher Clark, *Revolutionary Spring: Europe Aflame and the Fight for a New World, 1848–1849* (New York: Crown, 2023), 654–55.

Wagner would crib from in designing the Festspielhaus in Bayreuth, saw to the erection of "some of the handsomest and most elaborate barricades seen anywhere in revolutionary Europe."[34] Wagner is believed to have assisted Röckel in obtaining grenades and certainly did service as a lookout. Bakunin had a well-loved stand of trees chopped down.

The provisional government could dispose of thousands of armed men, but its support was not so broad as to include the Saxon army. Prussia, now determined to establish order and assert its importance in German affairs, sent its own forces, and on May 9, in a day of fighting, the two armies crushed the rebellion. At least two hundred fifty rebels were killed and around four hundred were wounded.[35] Röckel and Bakunin were captured and condemned to death. Both sentences were commuted, Bakunin was sent to Russia and then to Siberia, and Röckel was not released until the beginning of 1862. Wagner escaped, ending up in Zurich after a stay in Paris. He was not able to return to Germany until 1860, and Saxony was closed to him until 1862.

His major theoretical works were all fruits of this exile: *Art and Revolution* in France and *The Artwork of the Future, Opera and Drama,* and other texts in Switzerland. As we have already seen, these present a philosophy that goes well beyond their ostensible concern with aesthetics and with the interweaving of art and forms of social life. Through them, moreover, Wagner took a crucial step beyond the simplistic world view he had shared with Bakunin. His emphasis on the inevitability of error as an inherent element in self-consciousness allowed him to address some unavoidable political problems. Why had the revolution failed, not just in Saxony but everywhere? The European social order had seemed fragile and unstable. Poverty and hunger were common. The injustice of social and economic institutions was hard to ignore, the literate classes were fed up with censorship and the secret police, and popular discontent was widespread. Yet that social order turned out to be far more resilient than it looked, its armed defenders were happy to do their job and kill those who threatened it, and most of those who had manned barricades or argued passionately in the provisional parliaments were able to settle comfortably back into the status quo, fanatics like Bakunin excepted. In the long run many of the revolutionaries' more moderate demands were accepted into the liberal European order of the later nineteenth century, but that could hardly have been anticipated in the 1850s. From Wagner's

---

34 Clark, *Revolutionary Spring*, 253.
35 Clark, *Revolutionary Spring*, 253.

perspective the revolution had been a disaster, and the disaster called for explanations and analysis.

Bakunin could come up with none except the continent-wide use of violence against the public, but Wagner wanted and achieved something more illuminating than that. As he told Röckel years later, he had once thought that to make a better world "it was only necessary for man to wish it. I ingeniously set aside the problem, why they did not wish it."[36] He did not set it aside for long, however, and in fact he was working though that problem in the last major text he wrote in Dresden, a sketch for an opera on *Jesus of Nazareth* and the explanatory notes that accompany it.

Jesus of Nazareth is a key work in the development of Wagner's philosophical and political thinking. Its notes, especially, seem so influenced by Feuerbach's *Thoughts on Death and Immortality* that he may have been familiar with this text before his exile; his autobiographical account would be in error. All the same, Wagner goes well beyond Feuerbach, venturing into history, political theory, and even social psychology. He sets out a kind of philosophical history that traces a steady decline, starting with the Fall, that led to the tyranny of the state:

> God was one with the world from the beginning: the earliest races (Adam and Eve) lived and moved in this oneness, innocent, unknowing it: the first step in knowledge was the distinguishing between the helpful and the harmful; in the human heart the notion of the Harmful developed into that of the Wicked: this seemed to be the opposite of the Good, the Helpful, of God, and that dualism formed the basis of all Sin and Suffering of mankind.
>
> Human Society next sought deliverance through the Law: it fastened the notion of Good to the Law, as to something intelligible and perceptible by us all: but what was bound fast to the Law was only a moment of the Good, and since God is eternally generative, fluent and mobile, the Law thus turned against God's self; for, as man can live and move by none save the ur-law of Motion itself, in pursuance of his nature he needs must clash against the Law .... This is man's suffering, the suffering of God himself, who has not come as yet to consciousness in men.[37]

---

36 *Letters to August Roeckel*, 149 (August 23, 1856), *SL* 357. Wagner's elaboration that follows is so influenced by Schopenhauer that it "cannot be reconciled with the work itself" (Carl Dahlhaus, *Wagner's Music Dramas*, trans. Whittall [Cambridge: Cambridge University Press, 1979], 104; the entire discussion from 101 on is extremely valuable.)

37 Richard Wagner, *Jesus of Nazareth*, trans. Ellis, *PW* VIII, 311.

That suffering could be ended only by the abolition of "the distinction between the helpful and the harmful through our recognition that ... the two are the selfsame utterance of creative force." Once we see through the separation of self and world that self-consciousness requires, God and humanity would be seen as one, and the law "which opposed itself as State to Nature" would fall to the ground. Jesus' "proclamation of Love" was, at its heart, a call to realize that "the *only* God indwells in us and in our unity with Nature."[38] The echoes of Fichte and Bakunin here are unmistakable,[39] as are the anticipations of the significance of love as Wagner explained it to Röckel.

The Zurich texts elaborate these ideas within a broader context, opened up by Wagner's grasp of the inherent limits of self-consciousness, and they describe this historical process in more general and secular terms. In *Opera and Drama* it is developed through Wagner's idiosyncratic but perceptive analysis of Sophocles' *Oedipus Tyrannos* and *Antigone*. He portrayed Antigone as the perfect human being, a widely held view at the time,[40] but unlike Hegel, who saw her as caught between two sets of rights, Wagner placed her within a primordial conflict between the instinctive drive of the real and the inflexible ordering of the social. Through her self-sacrifice she exposed the contradictions within the Theban state and destroyed the tyranny of Creon,[41] but the problem at the root of her dilemma could not be resolved until both individual and society were seen to derive from the real, and until their conflict was seen to have been "grounded on an erroneous view of the essence of the Individual."[42]

Through his gloss on Sophocles Wagner argued that the inherent split between self-conscious humanity and nature had baleful historical and political consequences. It had led to a fixed and suffocating antagonism between the individual and the state, mediated though private property and founded on the denial of the creative and ever-changing reality accessible only through egoless love. Without a community rooted in natural necessity Fichtean ethical surrender of the ego was unappetizing or even impossible, leading not to self-realization but to self-denial. "In this world of egoistic yearning and dislike," Wagner had written in *Jesus of*

---

38 *Jesus of Nazareth, PW* VIII, 311.
39 It is more pantheism, different from Fichte's panentheism, but as Fichte's god is unknowable this difference is relatively unimportant.
40 See, generally, George Steiner, *Antigones* (New Haven, CT: Yale University Press, 1996). Steiner, unfortunately, does not address Wagner's analysis.
41 *Opera and Drama, PW* II, 190. These themes are developed further in chapter 7, below.
42 *Opera and Drama, PW* II, 180.

Nazareth, "man was to divest himself of his egoism in favour of a generality from which love, i.e. the blessed consciousness of love, had vanished—to wit, *Possession*."[43] He took this argument further in *The Artwork of the Future*, suggesting the social and psychological implications of an economy founded on private property and profit:

> This passion to hold fast to property, nail down each plank and beam of it for all eternity seems the only object worthy of human forethought and thus seeks to limit any possibility of future independent life, uprooting where possible its very self-determining life drive, the prick of its evil provocative thorns, to protect this property from all rough handling, according to the natural law of five per cent, in an inexhaustible round of the new generation and replacement of material to be chomped and gorged with self-satisfaction. ... [T]his great modern human preoccupation marks for all time the human being as profoundly weak or untrustworthy, kept only on the straight and narrow by property or laws.[44]

This is a fundamentally inhuman order, and in fact is the death of community. Instead of free citizens the population divides itself into elites and the masses whom "they must conceive ... as their own opposite," and Wagner reminds his (elite) readers that "all the vice and depravity that sickens you about the masses are nothing but the desperate symptoms of the struggle which true human nature is waging against its brutal oppressor, modern civilisation, and ... these appalling symptoms, far from being the true face of nature, reflect rather the false grotesque face of your state and police culture."[45]

But this culture is also fostered and maintained by a regressive, narcissistic nostalgia that Wagner had earlier seen as a response to the emptiness and repressive character of public life:

> The state of Innocence could not come to men's consciousness until they had lost it. This yearning back thereto, the struggle for its re-attainment, is the soul of the whole movement of civilization since ever we learnt to know the men of legend and of history. It is the impulse to depart from a generality that seems hostile to us, to arrive at egoistic satisfaction in ourselves. ... Only in joy at life can egoism willingly put off itself; if life itself is a joyless thing to me, in its increase and multiplication—the maintenance of this joyless state—I

---

43 *Jesus of Nazareth*, PW VIII, 321.
44 *The Artwork of the Future*, 83, PW I, 206.
45 *The Artwork of the Future*, 84, PW I, 207–8.

naturally can find no satisfaction, but wish myself back in the state of innocence, namely of inactive, unproductive egoism.⁴⁶

Real individuality is always social, something which "we win *alone within society*";⁴⁷ people make and remake themselves through each other. The passive, beleaguered egoism that Wagner saw was nothing like that, and in the absence of a free and living social world each person lived in isolation from all others and "the inexhaustible variety of the relations of living individualities to one another, exactly answering in their mutability the idiosyncrasy of these vital relations, we are not in a position to so much as conceive."⁴⁸ As a result, not even utopian dreaming could lead to anything different:

> Nothing has been more detrimental to human happiness than this insane zeal to build the future with the laws of the present; this revolting preoccupation with the future, in truth a function of gloomy, absolute egoism, is at root nothing but an attempt to conserve what we have today, to reassure us for our lifetime.⁴⁹

"Our own pitiful ineptitude," Wagner wrote, "drives us to create new laws for the future which we violently uphold to one basic end: that we may never become true artists, true human beings."⁵⁰ These laws are rarely needed, however. Our way of life is unassailable once we accept the chasm between individual and society. As long as we wear ourselves out seeking material security and busy ourselves with the rounds of daily life the troops can sleep soundly in their barracks. Our entertainments and projects promise to lead us back to the delights of infantile egoism, and when those fail there are always new transactional relationships, new amusements, new longed-for objects, and new shining futures, always dangled before us whenever we notice that the old ones have not delivered the joy they promised. We are free to do anything we want, just so long as it makes no difference.

In such a world "all progress is only conceivable as an artificial need, as a hunger aroused by stimulation; and this is in truth what lies behind the entire impulse of our contemporary culture."⁵¹ Human society is so far estranged from reality that the existence of the real cannot

46 *Jesus of Nazareth*, PW VIII, 320.
47 *Opera and Drama*, PW II, 195.
48 *Opera and Drama*, PW II, 203. Translation altered.
49 *The Artwork of the Future*, 83, PW I, 206.
50 *The Artwork of the Future*, 83, PW I, 206.
51 *The Artwork of the Future*, 20, PW I, 84.

even be thought, and anything that calls us to real life is terrifying. We retreat into the narrow life of the upright citizen and good consumer, who "constantly abides in egoism … [so] the movement of life … takes place against his will; what he wills, he cannot consummate, but what he wills not, he must see fulfilled on him: he therefore remains a sufferer till death."[52] Such lives are marked by what Wagner's almost-exact-contemporary Kierkegaard called the despair which is ignorant of being despair.[53]

Wagner was confronting the same impasse that Fichte had addressed in two of his most widely read books, *The Characteristics of the Present Age* and the often-misunderstood *Addresses to the German Nation*. He may or may not have been familiar with either work; he eventually acquired and kept a copy of the *Addresses*, but this was not until after he had finished the text of the *Ring*.[54] The similarities are striking, however, both in the way the problems are set out and in their conclusions for social and political action.

What Wagner calls reality or nature Fichte calls "Reason," by which he meant not discursive logic but his "one life," "the only possible and self-sustaining existence and life, of which all that seems to us to exist and live is but a modification, definition, variety, and form."[55] And just as Wagner insisted that we had estranged ourselves from the formative movement of nature, Fichte argued that we had estranged ourselves from Reason itself:

> Reason, in whatever shape it reveals itself, whether as instinct or as knowledge, always proceeds upon the life of the genus, as a genus;— Reason being thrown off and extinguished, nothing remains but the mere individual, personal life. Hence, in the [present] age, which has set itself free from Reason, there is nothing but this latter life; nothing wherever this age has thoroughly manifested itself and arrived at clearness and consistency, except pure, naked egoism.[56]

---

52   *Jesus of Nazareth*, PW VIII, 321.
53   Søren Kierkegaard, *The Sickness Unto Death*, trans. Hannay (London: Penguin, 1989), 73.
54   https://www.wagnermuseum.de/wp-content/uploads/2019/01/bestandsliste_wahnfried.pdf. This was the 1859 reedition.
55   Johann Gottlieb Fichte, "The Characteristics of the Present Age," in *The Popular Works of Johann Gottlieb Fichte*, vol. II, 21. I have removed Smith's italics and most of his capitalization.
56   Fichte, "The Characteristics of the Present Age," 65. Smith translated "Gattung" as "race," which is much more misleading today than it was in 1859, and I have altered the translation accordingly.

Many of Fichte's descriptions of this "Third Age" of humanity clearly anticipate Wagner's harshest critiques of contemporary culture, and it is hard not to believe that he had Fichte in mind in the passages quoted above and when he wrote, in *The Artwork of the Future*, that "[t]he period from this point in time to our present day is therefore the history of absolute egoism and the end of this period will be its redemption through communism."[57]

And both Fichte and Wagner agreed that the problem of effecting change arises from the reduction of the social to "mere individual, personal life." We have freed ourselves as individuals, but we are not individuals at all; we are equal co-participants in an ongoing movement of reason, nature, reality, or whatever you want to call it. Our crisis arises from the way our blinkered focus on the individual has cut us off from that movement, which it does so thoroughly that we either deny its existence or battle against it as an alien force. As Wagner argued, that battle, which is a civil war within ourselves, makes social life into a threat which drives us back into "inactive, unproductive egoism." It is also why Fichte, who had started with hope of changing the world, came close to despair: "Philosophy must require [our generation] to give up its present world and to provide itself with an entirely different one," he wrote. "It is no wonder if such a demand proves unavailing."[58]

How then can we reengage with reality, and reconnect our common lives to the activity that makes them both truly common and truly alive? This is the question at the core of Fichte's *Addresses to the German Nation*. His answer was not some proto-fascist nationalism but a new kind of national education, owing much to Rousseau and the educational reformer Pestalozzi, in which boys and girls would essentially educate each other.[59] They would form themselves into a community, and as a community they could bring forth images of what the world should be. In their love for that future world they would spontaneously go forth to reshape reality in its light.[60]

---

57 *The Artwork of the Future*, 63, *PW* I, 166–67.
58 Fichte, *Addresses to the German Nation*, 145.
59 The present discussion reworks and revises portions of Michael Steinberg, "How to Change the World: Cultural Critique and the Historical Sublime in the *Addresses to the German Nation*," in *Fichte's "Addresses to the German Nation" Reconsidered*, ed. Daniel Breazeale and Tom Rockmore (Albany: SUNY Press, 2016), 223–42.
60 Fichte, *Addresses to the German Nation*, 103, 238.

It was essential to that process that the students be isolated from their parents, because we ourselves cannot make that world. We can only spoil those who could have made it:

> If we possess one spark of love for [our children], we must remove them from our foul atmosphere and build a more salubrious abode for them [and] we must not let the children back from this society into our own until ... they have learned to loathe the full extent of our corruption and are thereby rendered completely immune to any contamination.[61]

Our own visions of things have no authority or value; "To see differently," as Fichte cautions, "you would have to become different from what you are."[62] As Wagner knew as well, our dreams of the future are all founded on our own ideas, and they can do nothing but "conserve what we have today."

We have to remove ourselves from the equation, then. Wagner saw this clearly and made it into one of the central themes of the *Ring*. He wrote to Röckel, speaking of Wotan as the Wanderer:

> Look well at him, for in every point he resembles us. He represents the actual sum of the Intelligence of the Present, whereas Siegfried is the man greatly desired and longed for by us of the Future. But we who long for him cannot fashion him; he must fashion himself and by means of our annihilation.[63]

He did not mean collective suicide, of course, but an abstention born of the understanding that we cannot see beyond our own limitations.

That Wagner did not participate in revolutionary politics after 1849 does not mean that he had turned away from the task of changing the world. Not even Schopenhauer could do that. Instead, he had come to see that conventional or even revolutionary ideas of a transformed way of life were never revolutionary enough. They all took their departure from the ideas of the present, which were so deeply embedded that if we started there we could never shape a genuinely human and humane world.

Since we could not chart the way forward, what was left for us to do is to carry out the kind of creative destruction that Marx described to Arnold Ruge, his friend and Bakunin's, as well: "If we have no business

---

61 Fichte, *Addresses to the German Nation*, 216–17.
62 Fichte, *Addresses to the German Nation*, 157.
63 *Letters to August Roeckel*, 100–101 (January 25–26, 1854), *SL* 308.

with the construction of the future or with organizing it for all time there can still be no doubt about the task confronting us at present: the *ruthless criticism of the existing order.*"[64] It was in this spirit that Wagner transformed the straightforward grand opera of *Siegfrieds Tod* into the many-voiced music dramas of the *Ring*. He began with heroic tragedy and ended by putting everything in question.

---

64 Karl Marx, "Letter to Arnold Ruge of September, 1843," trans. Livingstone and Benton in Marx, *Early Writings* (New York: Vintage Books, 1975), 207.

5: From *Siegfrieds Tod* to *Der Ring des Nibelungen*

It is often said that the *Ring* was written backwards and composed forwards. This is not far from the truth, but the reality is, as always, more complicated than the quip. It is true that Wagner originally wrote the text for a single opera, *Siegfrieds Tod*, the first version of what would ultimately become *Götterdämmerung*. He then realized that *Siegfrieds Tod* could not stand alone, so he wrote a prequel, *Der junge Siegfried*, which in its final form became *Siegfried*. That did not solve the problem, either. Audiences would still have needed a good deal of background information to make sense of what was going on, and imparting this verbally was apt to be confusing or tedious and would carry too little emotional weight; as Wagner wrote to Liszt, "a work of art ... can only make its rightful impression if the poetic intent is fully presented to the senses in every one of its important moments."[1] Events conveyed through narrative would not work well with Wagner's evolving language of musical-dramatic motifs and their development, either, as Carl Dahlhaus explains:

> Anything that had no foundation in the action was suspect to Wagner. ... In order to be understood beyond all shadow of doubt ... a musical idea—a "melodic element"—had to be introduced in association with both words and an event on the stage, and it was the latter that was of crucial importance. ... It is only when a musical motive has been explicitly associated with something on the stage, with the gold, the ring, Valhalla or the restraints placed on Wotan by his contracts and obligations ... that it can become a motive of remembrance or a leitmotiv: a means, that is, of linking what is seen and spoken with what is not seen and not spoken.[2]

To say anything about the Ring he had to show everything, and that is why one music drama became four. As he expanded the project, though, his original vision turned into something quite different.

---

1   Letter to Franz Liszt, November 20, 1851, *SL*, 237.
2   Dahlhaus, *Wagner's Music Dramas*, 85–86.

Wagner had, in fact, sketched something akin to the entire story of the *Ring* before he had turned any of it into dramatic form. He finished that prose outline, *The Nibelung Myth as Draft for a Drama,* on October 4, 1848, and by the end of November he had completed the versified text for *Siegfrieds Tod.*[3] Then came the Dresden uprising, exile, and the major prose works. He did not pick up the *Ring* project again until May, 1851, when he started the first prose sketch for *Der junge Siegfried*. By the end of June he had a verse draft of this work, and by May, 1852, he had prose treatments for *Das Rheingold* and *Die Walküre*, written in that order. The versification of these went in reverse order, though, first *Die Walküre* and then *Das Rheingold*. These were done by November 3, 1852, and by mid-December he had revised the last two dramas to make them consistent with the first two.

All of this writing and rewriting was also a rethinking, an exploration of what had lain hidden within Wagner's first ideas about a Nibelung opera and which came to shape the final version of the *Ring*. That process was a parallel to something John Deathridge saw in the drafts of the orchestral conclusion to *Götterdämmerung*:

> The first draft of the ending, in its final form one of the greatest moments in musical theater, is perhaps one of the most disconcerting documents in the Bayreuth archives. If one takes an uncharitable view of musical composition, it could have been written by a roughly trained university student doing a paper in tonal composition. And indeed there is no better proof than the difficult journey from this to the magnificent final version of Thomas Mann's remark about Wagner's dilettante traits, which, he claimed, were raised miraculously with enormous effort to the level of genius.[4]

Mann's insight also comes to mind when looking at the extraordinary development of Wagner's project from the 1848 prose sketch to the 1853 poems, which were identical in most respects to the ones he was to set to music over the next twenty years. Wagner's genius was indeed receptive, but it took years of hard work before he could hear what the mythos of the Nibelungs and the Norse gods had to say to him.

---

3   This information is from the chronology in Nattiez, *Wagner Androgyne,* 9–10. Wagner's usual procedure was to write a brief prose sketch followed by a detailed prose draft, a verse draft, and the more-or-less-final poem. He was meticulous in preserving these and dating them.

4   John Deathridge, *Wagner Beyond Good and Evil* (Berkeley: University of California Press, 2008), 96.

In the portion of the 1848 *Nibelung Myth* that corresponds to *Die Walküre*, for example, Wotan's only connection with the birth of Siegmund and Sieglinde is a gift of one of Freia's golden apples to a childless Volsung couple. Both twins born of that gift marry and both marriages are barren, so "in order to bring forth a true Volsung, brother and sister come together themselves. Hunding ... finds out about the crime, exiles his wife, and attacks Siegmund."[5] Wotan appears to be just as angry with the Volsungs as Hunding is—there is no mention of Fricka— and he condemns Siegmund to die "to atone for his crime."[6] Brünnhilde protects Siegmund, although the sketch does not explain why she does this, the hero's sword is shattered by Wotan's spear, and from then on the sketch proceeds much as in Act Three of the final version.

Nothing of what we treasure in *Die Walküre* is present in this sketch. There is no suffering wife of an abusive husband, no forlorn warrior, and no love between the Volsung twins; their coupling resembles stock-breeding more than anything else. Wotan does not have to bear Fricka's reproaches, he is not trapped between his contractual obligations and his fear of the power of the Ring, and he has no emotional relationship with his daughter, if indeed Brünnhilde *is* his daughter; in the Norse sources the Valkyries are not biological children of Wotan/Odin, and Brünnhilde is never identified or described that way in either the sketch or *Siegfrieds Tod*. An opera that did no more than show these events would have been emotionally and dramatically inert, and it would have closed with a farewell scene that carried little more pathos than a plea negotiation.

Even the individual prose sketches and drafts of the early 1850s can be appallingly unfocused. The first sketch for *Das Rheingold*, for example, has Wotan learn about the gold's properties as he is bathing in the Rhine, something which Warren Darcy writes had "mercifully" disappeared by the time Wagner scribbled some additional notes in a pocket notebook.[7] The prose sketches for *Die Walküre* contain no such howlers, and they are a significant advance on the 1848 account, but for quite some time Wagner seemed obsessed with bringing Wotan onstage in the first act. He was slow to see what a mistake this would have been.

In Wagner's initial sketch Wotan enters "as a stranger" as Siegmund, Sieglinde, and Hunding are having dinner; "he thrusts a sword into

---

5 Translation by Edward Haymes in *Wagner's Ring in 1848* (Rochester, NY: Camden House, 2010), 47–49.

6 Haymes, *Wagner's Ring in 1848*, 49. She is mentioned in *Siegfrieds Tod*, but not in a way that suggests any antagonism between the gods: 96–97.

7 Warren Darcy, *Das Rheingold* (Oxford: Clarendon Press, 1993), 39, 41.

the ash-tree. Siegmund pulls it out. Sieglinde senses that he must be a Volsung."[8] The final sketch is similar, but then, in a marginal note, Wagner changed everything having to do with the sword, realizing that "the story of the sword provides the opportunity for [Sieglinde] to tell her own story."[9] As Cooke notes, this improves the drama in several ways. It allows the act to end with the *coup de théâtre* of Nothung's being pulled from the tree. Wotan now appears only as a war god, making his abandonment of his children more comprehensible. Siegmund's unawareness of the sword heightens his desperation, and Sieglinde's narration, one of the most moving passages in the score, brings home her victimization by Hunding and the other men of his clan.

Other changes show a rethinking that goes beyond mere theatrical technique. Darcy notes that in the prose drafts for *Das Rheingold* "there is, amazingly, no mention of Wodan's spear! ... Considering the symbolic and musical ramifications of the spear, its complete absence in the prose draft is truly astonishing."[10] But Wagner was no Jungian, and he would never have assumed that certain shapes or objects had inherent meaning. He was not leaving out something with great "symbolic and musical" significance. Wotan's spear is just a pointed stick until we see what he does with it and how characters respond to its use and its user. He does have a spear in the *Nibelung Myth* sketch; he shatters Siegmund's sword with it. But it is a weapon and nothing more, part of the traditional iconography of Wotan/Odin like the rams that pull Fricka's chariot. This was to change, but the change was slow in coming.

Up until the summer of 1852 Wotan's spear "was of virtually no importance" in the dramas, as Daniel Coren wrote:

> In *Der junge Siegfried*, Wotan is described as carrying it with him into Mime's cave in Act I, but Wagner never refers to it again in the stage directions, nor does Wotan so much as mention its powers. As Wagner wrote the *Walküre* and *Rheingold* poems, the spear became an extremely powerful symbol. ..., simultaneously a symbol of restraint embodied in law, and a literal weapon. In the finished *Ring*, it is an omnipresent reminder of Wotan's basic condition, a condition that combines irresistible strength and final impotence.[11]

---

8   In Cooke, *I Saw the World End*, 293.

9   Cooke, *I Saw the World End*, 294.

10 Darcy, *Das Rheingold*, 43. Wotan is called "Wodan" in the drafts, but for simplicity's sake I have used the final spelling throughout, just as I have omitted the apostrophe that Wagner used for some years in the title *Siegfrieds Tod*.

11 Daniel Coren, "The Texts of Wagner's *Der junge Siegfried* and *Siegfried*," *19th-Century Music* 6, no. 1 (1982): 25.

In the first poetic version of *Der junge Siegfried*, Coren adds, the spear does not figure in the confrontation between Wotan and his grandson, and the scene is not even very confrontational: "Siegfried does not treat his grandfather with the rudeness that rouses Wotan in *Siegfried*, nor does Wotan lose his self-control when Siegfried becomes impatient to continue on his way. ... When Siegfried is predictably unshaken by Wotan's description of the fire, the Wanderer cedes to him and simply fades away—literally."[12]

It was only when working on the versified text for *Die Walküre* that Wagner began to think of the spear as a symbol; only then did he begin to build up the complex associations that surround it in the cycle as a whole, and—most importantly—to identify Wotan and the spear with a contract- or law-based political order. It is in *Das Rheingold*, the last of the verse texts to be written, where Wagner has Fricka and even Fasolt remind Wotan that his authority depends on the contracts inscribed on its shaft, and where he has Wotan himself brandishing it to prevent Donner's threatened violence against the giants.

These resonances allow key moments of the Ring to work on multiple levels. In *Die Walküre* the spear is the instrument of law against which Siegmund is powerless. In *Siegfried*, by contrast, it is the law that fails. When Wotan stops his grandson on the way to Brünnhilde's rock and, holding it out, boasts of it as "the symbol of lordship" which had shattered Nothung, Siegfried recognizes him as his father's enemy and delights in the prospect of revenge.[13] Nothung, "reborn" at Siegfried's hands, easily cuts the spear in two. This symbolic killing inverts the action of Act Two in *Die Walküre*, but it is also the end of an epoch, the passage from the age of the gods to that of humanity. Both meanings rely on the associations that Wagner had woven around the spear through dialogue, dramatic action, and motivic references. Neither would be possible if it had remained nothing more than a spear.

We are used to thinking of the *Ring* as a drama of all-encompassing significance. That was what Wagner ultimately intended, but the cosmic meaning of his dramas, like the meaning of the spear, was not so much planned as it was discovered. As he wrote to Röckel:

> I was scarcely aware that in the working out, nay, in the first elaboration of my scheme, I was being unconsciously guided by a wholly different, infinitely more profound intuition.[14]

12 Coren, "The Texts of Wagner's *Der junge Siegfried* and *Siegfried*," 25.
13 *S* III, lines 2325 ff.
14 *Letters to August Roeckel*, 150 (August 23, 1856), *SL* 357–58.

He went on to explain that he had unknowingly "grasped the very essence and meaning of the world itself in all its possible phases, and had realized its nothingness"; this was in 1856, after his "conversion" to Schopenhauer's philosophy. That conversion was arguably only skin-deep, however, and there are good reasons to set aside the pessimism with which Wagner clothed his thought.[15] It is hard, though, to doubt his sense of surprise.

Siegfrieds Tod looks a lot like *Götterdämmerung*, and Wagner's alterations may seem minor. They are not. The development of one work into the other is as astonishing as it is revealing, and so is Wagner's economy of means. A comparison of the two, though, does more than inspire respect or admiration, especially when the revisions are seen as parts of the larger reworking of the *Nibelung Myth* into the four dramas of the *Ring*. It shows us Wagner transforming a conventionally heroic opera about the expungement of a specific wrong into something truly extraordinary and philosophically impressive: a vision of gods and humans striving in vain to hold together an irreparably broken world.

There is nothing fundamentally flawed with the world of *Siegfrieds Tod* or *The Nibelung Myth*. The gods are "high-minded," they govern through "wise laws," and they have "the most solicitous care" for humanity.[16] They bear little resemblance to the quarrelsome, short-sighted, and sometimes oafish gods of *Das Rheingold*. Wotan does not bargain away Freia to get Valhalla built, and in fact she is never mentioned in the prose sketch. Instead, he shortsightedly allows the builders to name their price: "after finishing its construction the giants demand the hoard of the Nibelungs," and the gods dutifully employ their "superior intelligence" to obtain it.[17] Shaw warned against the "danger" of thinking "that the gods, at least, are a higher order than the human order. On the contrary, the world is waiting for Man to redeem it from the lame and cramped government of the gods."[18] This is not what Wagner was thinking when he wrote the *Nibelung Myth*, however. The gods in that text were essentially the tutors or kind parents of humanity. Their sole flaw was their mishandling of the Ring, which left the Nibelungs in slavery.

Perhaps it would be better to leave "Ring" uncapitalized, though, because we will not understand its significance in those texts if we think

---

15 Some of these are set out in the Appendix, below.
16 Haymes, *Wagner's Ring in 1848*, 46–47.
17 Haymes, *Wagner's Ring in 1848*, 44–45.
18 George Bernard Shaw, *The Perfect Wagnerite* (New York: Dover, 1967), 29.

of all the associations and implications that surround it in the final ones. A ring is merely a small metal hoop. Like Wotan's spear and the other symbols in the *Ring*, it must be defined through action, through its uses and the ways in which others covet or fear it.

Wagner's first conception of the ring turns out to have little in common with the Ring of the *Ring* cycle, where it is the symbol and vehicle of absolute dominion. In *Das Rheingold* this is clearly explained at the outset, when Woglinde, introducing two of the most pregnant musical motifs of the entire tetralogy, tells Alberich and us that the world will be the inheritance of whoever forges from the Rhinegold the ring which gives him measureless power.[19] The price of this power is, of course, the renunciation of love.

In the 1848 texts, though, there is no mention of love or its renunciation, and the ring itself does not grant anyone "measureless power." In the *Nibelung Myth* Alberich steals the gold, and "with great cunning and art" forges "a ring which gave him the highest power over his whole race, the Nibelungs." They become his slaves, and he forces them to gather up "the immeasurable hoard of the Nibelungs" and forge the tarnhelm. "[E]quipped with those things, Alberich sought lordship over the earth and everything contained therein."[20] In *Siegfrieds Tod*, in the prologue's short, expository Norn scene, the first Norn says, "Alberich stole the Rhinegold, forged a ring, bound his brothers with it,"[21] and in his second-act nocturnal scene with Hagen Alberich tells his son that

> Through [the ring's] magical controlling power
> I tamed the industrious folk [of the Nibelungs] …
> The mighty horde I piled up so;
> It was supposed to gain me the world.[22]

The German text makes it clear that "it" in the last line refers to the horde, not to the ring. In Wagner's first version, then, the power of the ring was limited to the Nibelung race, and Alberich uses it to amass wealth and weaponry for a battle against the gods: Ragnarök, the Norse Armageddon which Wotan fears but which never occurs. If the ring gave

---

19 *R*, lines 262–66. It is difficult to render the complexity of Wagner's grammar into fluent English. The Woodbird, too, tells Siegfried that possession of the Ring will make him ruler of the world, *S* II, lines 1624–25.
20 Haymes, *Wagner's Ring in 1848*, 44–45.
21 Haymes, *Wagner's Ring in 1848*, 66–67.
22 Haymes, *Wagner's Ring in 1848*, 110–11.

him "measureless power" over all beings he would not have needed to take such an indirect route to world domination.[23]

This strategy fails, as it does in *Das Rheingold*, too. Alberich loses the gold and the ring to the gods, who use both to pay off the giants for building Valhalla, and the giants plod offstage. (They are unnamed at this stage and there is no Fafner/Fasolt murder.) Neither they not the gods have any care for the Nibelungs. The ring, symbolizing "the soul, the freedom of the Nibelungs,"[24] is buried under the dragon-guard employed by the giants, and this leaves both "the Nibelungs and Alberich ... in subjugation."[25] "Out of the depths of Nibelheim groans the knowledge of [the gods'] guilt: for the slavery of the Nibelungs has not been broken."[26]

At the end of *Siegfrieds Tod* Brünnhilde tells the Nibelungs that they are now free, as is Alberich.[27] Their oppression was the sin that had tarnished the gods' reign, and Siegfried's calling was to take that sin upon himself and to redeem it with his freely offered death. But here, it must be confessed, Wagner's early treatments of the story had become hopelessly confused. Siegfried does not offer himself for slaughter, he is murdered, and why he has to die is unclear; the ring is useful only to order the Nibelungs around, and it could simply have been returned to the river. Wagner seems to have been led into a dead end because of an obsession with the idea of vicarious atonement. That notion would seem unavoidable if one is writing about Jesus, as he did right after the first two Nibelung pieces, but Wagner ducks the issue there, and to make sense of it in any context—a tall order, actually—there must be a higher authority which demands punishment and which is willing to treat suffering as fungible, accepting one person's death as payment for another's sin.[28] This

---

23 There remain some relics of this in the final text; in *Das Rheingold* Alberich does not even try to use the Ring against the gods, and his long-term plans closely resemble his 1848 ones: R, lines 1198 ff., 1230–32. The Ring nonetheless presents a much broader threat, which is why Wotan is so desperate to hold on to it, and he tells Brünnhilde that if Alberich regained it he could force the heroes of Valhalla to fight against him: W II, lines 1014–18. Cooke's gloss, that Alberich would accomplish this through bribery, eliminates the discrepancy but seems inconsistent with the coercive meaning of *zwängen*, the verb Wagner uses. Cooke, *I Saw the World End*, 331, fn. 10.
24 Haymes, *Wagner's Ring in 1848*, 46–47.
25 Haymes, *Wagner's Ring in 1848*, 44–45.
26 Haymes, *Wagner's Ring in 1848*, 46–47.
27 Haymes, *Wagner's Ring in 1848*, 182–83.
28 As the passages cited above from the *Jesus of Nazareth* show, Wagner had no concept of original sin, and Jesus' sacrifice was more a moral exemplar than an act of atonement.

is the Christian version, and elements of a similar scapegoating function can be seen in Greek tragedy, but in both cases the guilt that must be expunged is a human failing and the higher authority is divine. In the early Nibelung texts the gods accept human payment for their own sins, not for human ones, and that is a different thing altogether.

Logical coherence side, Siegfried's death not only does away with the ring which bound the Nibelungs, it ends the guilt of the gods, and they can continue their high-minded nurturing of the human race. "Let only one rule," proclaims Brünnhilde before she dives into Siegfried's funeral pyre to scoop him up and carry him to Valhalla: "All-father! Magnificent one!"[29] She is not announcing Wotan's sovereignty; that had never been in doubt. She is telling him that he no longer has to deal with the pretensions of any upstarts. Alberich was merely a feudal baron or *nouveau riche* who has now been put in his place, and Wotan is once again free to rule as an enlightened despot or, perhaps, as the republican monarch whom Wagner had briefly hoped would ally himself with the people and break the power of the aristocracy.

All this has changed in the *Ring* cycle itself. That Ring grants absolute power and works absolute evil, poisoning the lives of all who hold it, Siegfried and Brünnhilde not excepted, yet nobody can bring themselves to give it away. Siegfried's vicarious suffering plays no part in the action. The gods must pay for their own guilt, and it is Brünnhilde, not Siegfried, who does "the deed that redeems the world."[30] Her characterization in *Götterdämmerung* is correspondingly stronger than it is in *Siegfrieds Tod*, something which appears most strikingly in her imperious stubbornness in the 1852 scene with Waltraute compared with the 1848 conversation with the other Valkyries, where she begs for mercy and calls herself "the lost one."[31]

So the 1848 ring is not the 1852 Ring. The 1848 Wotan is not the Wotan of 1852, either, and Wagner's development of the god's character reveals a great deal about what he was discovering within his material. In the early texts, in fact, Wotan has no defined character at all. He is little more than an abstract authority symbol, bringing the force of law down on Siegmund and Brünnhilde, and neither he nor his rule comes in for

---

29   Haymes, *Wagner's Ring in 1848*, 182–83. The same language appears in *The Nibelung Myth*, also in Haymes, *Wagner's Ring in 1848*, 58–59.

30   *S* III, line 2146. This is perhaps the time to lay to rest the notion that Erda was some kind of divine brood cow who gave birth to all of the Valkyries. She and Wotan had only one daughter, Brünnhilde; see Barry Millington, "Myths and Legends," in *The Wagner Compendium*, ed. Barry Millington (London: Thames & Hudson, 1992), 136–37. The other Valkyries are half-sisters at most.

31   Haymes, *Wagner's Ring in 1848*, 98–99.

any criticism. The Wotan in the *Ring* itself is completely different. He is a complicated, equivocal, and fascinating character, and for many viewers and commentators he is the protagonist of the entire cycle.[32]

Yet we are apt to miss out on his real importance if we focus too much on Wotan as a tragic hero and on his inner and outer struggles. As Wagner's philosophical stance demands, we must also look at what underpins and shapes overt thoughts and intentions, and what Wotan wants and how he explains himself to himself should not distract us from what he is and what he does. These turn us away from personal drama, moving and important though that is, towards some of the fundamental problems that the action of the *Ring* works through and either resolves or fails to resolve. Wagner's increasing fascination with Wotan led him beyond his initial idea of providing a visually and musically graspable back story for *Siegfrieds Tod*. He found himself overlaying a narrative centered on the Ring with a separate but parallel narrative about Wotan and his world order. In 1848 he had one story to tell. By 1853 he was telling two stories at once, and this accounts, at least in part, for the *Ring*'s richness and complexity.

Even when these two stories proceed independently, as they often do, their interrelationships and narrative echoes create a sense of depth which a single linear narrative could never evoke, and Wagner developed a system of correspondences through which one illuminates the other. Wotan and Alberich are each other's nemesis and are protagonists in their own right, but they are also spiritual brothers, mirror images. It takes Cooke almost a full page to chart out their similarities,[33] but Wotan himself makes the connection explicit, calling himself Light-Alberich and the dwarf Dark-Alberich.[34] Neither can secure the Ring through his own powers, so both work through families. Wotan fathers the Volsungs, and they have a half-sister in Brünnhilde. Alberich fathers Hagen, who has half-siblings in the Gibichungs. And both rely on an object that they have torn away from the totality of things, a breach in the natural order that turns part of it against itself and which secures domination at the cost of killing what it dominates. This is obviously the case with the Ring. It is less obvious in the case of the spear, and through most of the cycle Wagner lulls us into going along with Wotan's own view of himself. We see his weapon as a

---

[32] Dahlhaus does not make this distinction, and in his discussion of the 1848 texts calls Wotan "lord of contracts." This is an anachronism; the contract-theme is not present in the earlier texts and likely does not predate Wagner's development of the spear as its expression in 1852. Dahlhaus, *Richard Wagner's Music Dramas*, 88.

[33] Cooke, *I Saw the World End*, 159.

[34] *S* I, lines 520, 562.

symbol and vehicle of a flawed but essentially benign power, and although there are a few hints to the contrary in the first three dramas, it is not until the Norns appear in the prologue of *Götterdämmerung* that we are told the terrible truth.

The Norns respect Wotan, and they praise the honesty of his contracts,[35] but before they do that the First Norn had already revealed the price of his actions:

> ... Wotan broke off
> from the world ash-tree a bough ...
> In the course of many years
> the gash drained the forest's strength;
> leaves fell, yellowed and dull,
> the tree rotted, arid and starved;
> the spring's waster
> dried up in distress.[36]

Since Wotan's authority comes from the contracts inscribed on his spear, this was either his first act as king of the gods or the precondition for his acts in that role. In the long run it was utterly destructive. We do not need to know anything about the world ash-tree besides its name; that alone tells us that what Wotan killed was life itself. He did not intend this, and, like the audience, he does not become aware of the damage he has done until much later, but his power cannot be disentangled from the fatal act on which it was founded. His spear thus acquires another layer of meaning. It is the symbol of a world torn away from reality and from the creativity and fecundity of nature itself.[37] The *Ring* depicts that world and shows that it must come to an end.

There is no all-encompassing critique in the first versions of the Nibelung story. There is in the *Ring* cycle, though, and it is brought home through its dual narratives and the structural echoes between Alberich and Wotan and between the dwarf's Ring and the god's spear. We recoil from the tyranny which the Ring symbolizes, but in his finished poems Wagner shows us that the promise of order held out by the gods is just a kinder, gentler form of control and is just as clearly founded on self-destructive violence. As Wotan himself recognized, he and his enemy

---

35   *G*, lines 44–47.

36   *G*, lines 25–36, translation altered from that given by John Deathridge in Richard Wagner, *The Ring of the Nibelung* (London: Penguin Random House, 2018).

37   That this separation from nature and reality may be inevitable would not make its consequences any less disastrous.

are both Alberichs. For Dark-Alberich, the dwarf, life was empty, and that seemed to permit the pursuit of arbitrary power; he stole the Rhinegold for evil or even pathological reasons. Wotan, Light-Alberich, promised peace and justice, but he could work only through an assemblage of contracts, alliances of individuals who were "profoundly weak or untrustworthy, kept only on the straight and narrow by property or laws,"[38] and to build this artificial and life-denying construct he killed the world ash-tree. Unlike Dark-Alberich, Light-Alberich acted from noble motives. But that is, as lawyers say, ultimately a distinction without a difference. Wotan's world also begins with a crime, and it, too, is shadowed if not cursed by the circumstances of its birth.

---

38   *The Artwork of the Future*, 83, *PW* I, 206.

6: *Das Rheingold:* Separation and Order

Much of the philosophy of Wagner's time, and certainly his own, evokes and tries to make manifest a dynamic identity of unity and difference. For Wagner this is the interplay of a shared, primordial necessity with its splintered reflection in individual experience; the first is ungraspable but is present as feeling, the second is present as conscious thought but can never escape the limits of self-consciousness. Neither can stand alone or be reduced to the other. They must be thought together.

It is that vision that dictates the very structure of Wagnerian music drama, which develops a unity-in-difference between poetry and music and between the actions and voices of the characters on stage and a continuously transforming orchestral fabric. These are essentially different reflections of an inexpressible oneness. The web of motivic development does not merely accompany the singers, but neither are the singers reduced to the status of extra color in the instrumental palette or additional threads in the orchestral tapestry. The poles are never merged. Instead, each one interacts with the other.

As Wagner wrote in *The Artwork of the Future*:

> The orchestra is, so to speak, the bedrock of endless, collective feeling out of which the individual feeling of the single performer may grow to its fullest breadth: it dissolves the solid, immovable ground of the real stage making it more or less fluid, pliable, impressionable, an ethereal surface whose unplumbable depths are those of the sea of feeling itself. Thus the orchestra resembles the earth, which as he stepped on it gave Antaeus renewed immortal vitality. Essentially the polar opposite of the performer's natural stage setting and therefore correctly placed outside the frame of the stage and sunk into the foreground, yet at the same time it completes this performance space by carrying the boundless element of physical nature into the no less boundless element of artistic human feeling until both envelop the performer in a kind of atmospheric ring that is both the natural and the artistic element.[1]

---

1   *The Artwork of the Future*, 75, *PW* I, 190–91.

Through the simultaneity of these two distinct elements, the "comprehensive line of human nature will manifest itself to the Feeling in a continuous, a mutually conditioning chain of moments of feeling ... of such strength and force of conviction, that the Action ... may issue from this wealth of conditions as their last instinctively demanded, and thus completely intelligible moment."[2] At the same time, though, the action is always comprehensible on its own terms.

Although the theory Wagner advances in *Opera and Drama* tends to give music a subordinate role, it is the orchestra that grounds us in the real, because it conveys

> ... the very thing which Word-speech in itself can *not* speak out, ... [t]hat which, looked at from the standpoint of our human intellect, is the Inexpressible. That this Inexpressible is not a thing unutterable per se, but merely unutterable through the organ of our Understanding; thus, not a mere fancy, but a reality,—this is shewn plainly enough by the Instruments of the orchestra themselves.[3]

It seems fitting, then, that the *Ring* cycle should begin with an orchestral evocation of primordial unity. Just about everyone who writes about the astonishing opening of *Das Rheingold* agrees, in essence, with Thomas Mann, who called it "the mythus of music itself, a myth-philosophy, a poem of music-creation."[4] Its 136 bars seem to grow organically from an immovable E flat that starts almost imperceptibly on the double-basses. The bassoons join them, at a perfect fifth above, and out of the harmonic series grows the first and most fecund of the major motifs of the score, the rising figure associated with nature itself, which is then elaborated to become the theme associated with the river Rhine. We are surely witnessing "a musical image of the elemental, the origin of things."[5]

The Rhinemaidens, too, seem part of an innocent, prelapsarian world. Their first lines are largely nonsense syllables, and even when they make sense their words are often expressive, not communicative. In their

---

2   *Opera and Drama*, PW II, 294.
3   *Opera and Drama*, PW II, 317. Translation altered; the word translated here as "inexpressible" can also mean "ineffable." Wagner, in a footnote, adds that this "explanation of the 'Unspeakable' ... might extend, perhaps not altogether wrongly, to the whole matter of Religious Philosophy."
4   Thomas Mann, "Richard Wagner and the *Ring*," in *Essays of Three Decades*, 368.
5   John Deathridge and Carl Dahlhaus, *The New Grove Wagner* (London: Macmillan, 1984), 149.

delight we seem to glimpse that wholeness from which we tear ourselves away to become self-aware human beings.

It is easy, then, to see Alberich's theft of the gold as that very act, the first moment of self-assertion; taking the gold from the riverbed would be a breach in the unity of reality itself. It is a crime, of course, but in a broader perspective it can appear to be something necessary, the *felix culpa* which makes human self-consciousness possible and which thus opens the path towards reality itself becoming self-aware. Donington calls it a Promethean act,[6] with the gold standing "for the true individuality which we all have within us but cannot possess in so far as we remain entangled in our unconscious longing to get back to 'paradise' as mother's boys or father's daughters." He maintains that what Alberich renounced "was not the love of woman. It was an undue dependence on the love of woman."[7]

The scene is much darker without Donington's rose-tinted Jungian spectacles, though, and what Alberich renounced is far more consequential. Love, for Wagner, is not to be confused with sensual pleasure or emotional companionship, as important as those are, and it is only inadequately summed up as Loge's "Weibes Wonne und Wert" ("women's loveliness and worth," in Deathridge's translation) or as Cooke's cozy "mutual love and fellowship."[8] As we saw earlier, it is a way of knowing and a vehicle of self-transformation. One cannot truly love without letting go of the ego and its self-drawn boundaries, and it is therefore through love that "we attain to the most perfect manifestation of reality"[9] and act spontaneously as the moral law would command. When Alberich cursed love, then, he cut himself off from any possible access to reality. He imprisoned himself within the limits of his own thoughts and feelings, armoring himself against the shared life he had renounced and which he could no longer acknowledge as his own. Ethical life became impossible, even unimaginable, and as a stranger in a strange land it would seem perfectly logical for him to treat everyone else as slaves.

His crime, though, is not the primordial act through which self-consciousness becomes possible. It came after that. That primordial act, the division between subject and object, is the origin of subjectivity, but it does nothing more than establish a standpoint. Alberich had gone farther,

---

6 Robert Donington, *Wagner's Ring and its Symbols* (London: Faber & Faber, 1969), 50.
7 Donington, *Wagner's Ring and its Symbols*, 47.
8 Cooke, *I Saw the World End*, 253.
9 *Letters to August Roeckel*, 86 (January 25–26, 1854), *SL* 304.

identifying his own existence with that standpoint, forging a self around it like a pearl grown around a bit of sand, and then rejecting anything that appeared to lie outside of it. This had all happened before the first E flat sounds in the double basses; from the moment he enters the scene Alberich is painfully self-aware and obsessed with his isolation. As the scene changes to the banks of the river, where Wotan sleeps dreaming among the flowers, we see just as clearly that the world of self-conscious individuals had long since come into being. Everything in the *Ring* cycle takes place within history, even its opening bars.

As impressive as they are, there is something misleading about the prelude and first scene of *Rheingold*. The beginning of the cycle is neither the beginning of the world nor the beginning of the story. In the 1848 versions it was at least the latter. Those texts were about the ring, how it was tied to the Nibelungs' bondage, how it acquired a curse, and how Siegfried's sacrifice freed Alberich and the other Nibelungs, expunged the curse, and eliminated the existential threat to the gods' beneficent rule. That narrative begins with Alberich, and his story coincides with the overall story. But Wagner's final text of the *Ring* has a wider reach. The Alberich narrative remains, but it takes second place to the narrative concerned with Wotan and the world-order he had instituted and enforces.[10] The Wotan narrative begins *in media res*, and within it the Ring itself, though anything but unimportant, functions as a problem that Wotan tries to solve but cannot.

That crisis will take him by surprise. At the beginning of *Das Rheingold* his dreams of eternal power and infinite glory are untroubled, and when he wakes he salutes Valhalla as the completion of his "eternal work." His is a kingdom for all time, or so he thinks. It is tempting to take him at his word. The contrast with Alberich makes his world-order look like the way things ought to be; Wotan is ruthless and unprincipled in Nibelheim, but Alberich is much worse, intent on enslaving men (and gods) and raping women.[11] He must be stopped, and if that demands the sacrifice of a few legalities and niceties we are happy to give Wotan a pass. The god's bad-faith bargain with the giants is harder to defend, but it is, after all, resolved by an agreed-upon amendment to its terms, and though both Fricka and Alberich get the best of him in their arguments

---

10 Alberich does nothing after uttering the curse except fathering Hagen, and the Ring is never used by any character. There is no textual basis for thinking that it has any ill effects on human society, either; Gunther has heard of it but is more interested in acquiring Brünnhilde as a wife. *G* I, lines 314–20.

11 *R*, lines 1221–24.

it is somehow Wotan who wins our sympathy. The way he is depicted in Kitcher and Schacht's *Finding an Ending* is almost hagiographical, and even critics such as Deryck Cooke will concede that without him "we might still be savages"; he expands on Wotan's own self-critique[12] to castigate him as "greedy for power, hypocritical, dreadfully cunning, brutally aggressive, and practically devoid of love," but grants that "there's one good thing about him: he has a noble ideal":

> Although there's nobody to force him, he rules, not entirely according to his own whims and desires, but to a large extent according to laws. His *own* laws, maybe, but nevertheless laws that have to be *honoured*—even, however deviously, by *himself*.[13]

This is harsher than the text warrants. Wagner always refers to the runes on the spear as contracts or treaties. These are records of agreements. They cannot be merely the product of Wotan's own will, then, and he loses his dispute with Fricka in Act Two of *Die Walküre* because he is bound by them *in spite of* his "whims and desires" and must follow their dictates categorically, not "deviously." That is why he calls himself the least free of beings.[14]

Whatever Wotan's personal flaws, the order he created and maintains rests on free consent, and it therefore seems like rationality and equality personified. That would be consistent with the way Wagner saw the story in 1848, when he portrayed the gods as good-intentioned if fallible, but by 1853 he had a different vision. Wotan's noble, contract-based order depends on a blinkered, atomized, and ultimately antihuman version of humanity.

Everyone reminds Wotan that his authority comes from the agreements recorded on his spear, so much so that Dahlhaus calls him the "lord of contracts,"[15] and we are likely to take its contractual order as familiar and self-evidently valid. Even though it is frequently no more than a legal fiction, the freedom and equality of contracting parties is one of the stereotypical markers of the modern world, often contrasted with the unequal obligations typical of feudalism.

Unlike laws, which are the utterances of a sovereign power, contracts are made by ordinary people, often with nothing more than a handshake. Yet Wagner reminds us that this is not something we can take at face value. Wotan's contracts are inscribed on a weapon, which he uses,

---

12 In *W* II, lines 919–25; the Norns are far more charitable.
13 Cooke, *I Saw the World End*, 267.
14 *W* II, line 888.
15 Dahlhaus, *Richard Wagner's Music Dramas*, 88.

ironically, to block Donner when he tries to attack the giants, at the same time telling his brother-in-law to do "Nothing by force!" Nothing, that is, but to keep others from using it. That privilege is Wotan's alone. He and Wagner both know that the monopoly of state power is the ultimate guarantor of contractual relations.

This is as true now as it was in the *Ring*. If I do not pay my debts I can be sued, and if I refuse to pay a judgment I can be jailed for contempt and the bailiffs or sheriff's deputies can break into my house, take away my belongings or even, in some cases, take possession of the house itself, selling everything at auction to pay my creditors. They can do this only because they are permitted to use force and I am not. This is a bit of reality we tend to ignore. We all assume that our bargains will be honored, but we pay little attention to the threat of violence on which that confidence rests. Wagner knew better. Agreements inscribed on a spear: one could hardly imagine a tidier or more vivid representation of the nature of contract law.

The reality, of course, is anything but tidy. One theme that runs through *Das Rheingold*, and is developed in *Die Walküre*, is the inevitable failure of contractual order. Wotan's rule is preferable to Alberich's, but it, too, is a breach in the inherent order of things, a constraint on the flow of life. The subjects of any contractual system are imagined to be discrete, sovereign individuals, not as different from Alberich as we would like to think. As Wagner said of his own time, their "community" is no more than a "confederacy of willful self-servers"[16] who trade away the fluid creativity of common life and replace it with politics and arms'-length exchanges which fix everything in place.[17] They themselves lose all genuine individuality, enacting and seeing only social roles, and the absence of any shared social grounding licenses sharp practice and exploitation of all kinds. Not only do ideas replace reality, property takes precedence over humanity. Yet the drives which generate and interconnect all things are constantly pushing against this free-for-all of winners and losers and its impoverished emotional life, and reality, natural necessity, finds expression "in tones of yearning and finally of revolt, and therefore in a tragic mood."[18]

It is not just the inflexibility of specific contracts, then, which limits and even throttles the life which Wotan struggles to manage. His

---

16 *The Artwork of the Future*, 23, *PW* I, 88.
17 A similar point is made in a very different way by *The Lego Movie*, where the existential threat is the "Kragl," or Krazy Glue.
18 *A Communication to my Friends*, *PW* I, 332. Ellis's translation here is one of his least helpful.

underlying problem is that he is trying to hold together an artificial order which is always prey to manipulation and is always being undermined by the real order which it denies. That is why it needs constant maintenance and repair, not to mention the occasional dose of repression.

As George Bernard Shaw knew, legal equality looks nice, but it should never be confused with real social equality. In *The Perfect Wagnerite,* the oldest book on the *Ring* still widely read and probably the most entertaining, he argued that Wagner had produced a full-blown allegory of nineteenth-century European society. In this interpretation Alberich is the Capitalist (Shaw himself tended to use capitalization) and the Nibelungs are the industrial proletariat. Wotan is both Church and State, Fricka, especially in the second act of *Die Walküre,* is State Law, and Loge, whom Shaw calls "Loki," is "Logic and Imagination, without living Will"[19] Siegfried is, of course, the Hero, of a "higher order" than the highest of the "three main orders of men."[20] He is the "Protestant" and a revolutionary on the model of "Bakoonin" who will put an end to capitalist exploitation. Shaw has more trouble with "Brynhild," but since he has to give her a role he makes her a vague personification of the hidden truth of religion, which Wotan and Loge have to put to sleep and conceal behind a fiery illusion, the magic fire being "the Lie that must, on the highest principles, hide the Truth."[21]

Shaw's "commentary" is both amusing and thought-provoking, but it is hopeless as an analysis of the cycle. It says more about its author's hobbyhorses and blind spots than it does about Wagner. Shaw is unsympathetic to everything Wagner means by love and has only scorn for what he calls "the love panacea." That is one reason his interpretation falls apart when Siegfried and Brünnhilde finally meet. (Characteristically, he does not reconsider his analysis but blames the "collapse of the allegory" on Wagner himself.) Even before then, however, he can only keep it going by ignoring or misrepresenting the work itself. For example, he has Loge employed "as dialectician in chief" after the curtain falls in *Das Rheingold*, indoctrinating the warriors brought to Valhalla by the Valkyries "with the conventional system of law and duty, supernatural religion and self-sacrificing idealism."[22] No imaginable reading of the text could justify this interpretation. Loge has no interest in propping up Wotan's authority,

---

19   Shaw, *The Perfect Wagnerite,* 28.
20   Shaw, *The Perfect Wagnerite,* 29.
21   Shaw, *The Perfect Wagnerite,* 40.
22   Shaw, *The Perfect Wagnerite,* 34.

and, cynic that he is, he is the last figure in the *Ring* who could be counted on to indoctrinate anyone.

As wrong-headed as he could be, though, Shaw was on to something. *Das Rheingold* is shot through with echoes of contemporary social structures and veiled references to contemporary economic issues. The Nibelungs are slaves, not wage workers, but the year after the first Bayreuth festival Wagner saw their subterranean world in industrial Britain: "This is Alberich's dream come true—Nibelheim, world dominion, activity, work, everywhere the oppressive feeling of steam and fog."[23] Mime, bound by the Ring to endless toil for Alberich's enrichment, laments "with a somewhat dance-like demeanor" the days when he and the other Nibelungs, laughing, had fashioned jewelry and other "dainty Nibelung playthings" for their wives;[24] what he tells Loge and Wotan suggests the brutal end of self-directed pre-industrial work and its flexible rhythms and the imposition of the relentless discipline and subjection to clock time demanded by the age of factories and capital accumulation.[25] Fasolt and Fafner are clear social types, worker aristocracy, perhaps, but workers all the same. They have contrasting responses to the pretensions of the ruling classes. One can almost see Fasolt, one of the few sympathetic characters in the drama, tugging at a forelock and telling Wotan: "Ye high and mighty folk have fine manners and got yerselves schooled at the best universities, and we working folk don't have none of yer advantages, but we still knows what's right and what ain't." His brother Fafner, on the other hand, is long past appealing to matters of principle or to anyone's better nature. He believes in neither of these. He just wants to burn the whole rotten system to the ground.

This is not to say that Wagner's dwarfs and giants are stock players or that the gods' superhuman roles are mere masks. This would fall into Shaw's major error, which is his insistence that the *Ring* is an allegory. It is not. An allegory is never fundamentally about its ostensible characters or events. It is always about something else, so it is meaningful only if its characters and events can be mapped onto a different story or network of relationships. Those unfamiliar with that territory need a crib sheet. Hawkers used to insist at baseball games that "you can't tell the players

---

23 Cosima Wagner, *Diaries*, vol. I, trans. Skelton (New York: Harcourt Brace Jovanovich, 1978), 965.
24 R, lines 1040–41, Deathridge's translation, which includes Wagner's 1876 comment. One thing that Wagner carries over from the 1848 texts is that the gods have no sympathy at all for the Nibelungs or their suffering.
25 The classic paper on this is E. P. Thompson, "Work-Disciple and Industrial Capitalism," *Past & Present* 38 (1967): 56–97, but it is hardly a controversial thesis.

without a program," but in an allegory most of us can't even understand the action without one. We need to rely on footnotes.

Wagner, by contrast, struggled to ensure that the *Ring* could be fully understood on its own terms. That is one reason for its extraordinary scale; it took four dramas to make everything clear. No significant character is without her or his motives. The action is propelled from within, starting with its characters' responses to the conditions in which they find themselves and growing deeper and wider as they struggle with the interweaving consequences of their acts. Wagner never treats them as straightforward personifications of ideas or social roles, and if he had done that he would have turned his back on his most cherished ideas about the calling of art.[26]

But he will not cut them off from their social and political grounding. The contemporary parallels are nowhere as overt in the next two dramas, and the echoes of Wagner's own time in *Götterdämmerung* are of a different nature, but they are certainly intentional. They indicate to the audience that the drama is not just some tale of old, unhappy, far-off things. Our world has no gods, giants, or dwarfs, but it is inhabited by people who play many of the same roles and have many of the same motivations. As Wagner insisted, the poet has "to show his characters at first in living situations having a recognizable likeness with such as we have found, or at least might have found, ourselves in; only from such a foundation, can he mount step by step to situations whose force and wondrousness remove us from the life of everyday, and show us humanity in the highest fullness of its power."[27]

In the *Ring*, at least, one level does not succeed the other. That its characters are both giants and divinities, on the one hand, and factory workers and CEOs on the other, both leads us into its action and has us exercise a kind of double vision. It catches us up in a dialectic of personal drama and myth which mirrors the interplay of character and fate and, ultimately, the interplay of the incomprehensible activity of the real with the psychological drives and aspirations which self-conscious beings take to be their own true nature. It exhibits both the elements of that dialectic and their underlying identity.

Wagner's plotting thus mirrors the unity-in-duplicity of the idealist vision. Bernard Williams suggested that he "took myths ... and instilled in them a psychology which is often that of bourgeois

---

26 This is also Bell's problem in treating it as a Christian allegory in *The Theology of Wagner's Ring Cycle*.
27 *Opera and Drama*, PW II, 338–39.

domestic drama."[28] This may create problems, but it is surely what Wagner intended. Wotan's career, for instance, must play out the mythic and political consequences of a primordial breach of the natural order, exhibit his own order's inherent limitations and its contingent challenges, and bring him from youthful impetuosity through armored ruler to renunciate, all within the same process.

That process is already underway in *Das Rheingold*. It is often easy to forget that its overt "story" is the gods' move from the earth to the heavens, and that this is also a movement from connection to separation, from openness to enclosure, and from agreements to militarization. At our first glimpse of Wotan he is sleeping unguarded in a bed of flowers. Through the drama's action we see him wheeling and dealing, betraying a hint of desperation now and then, and we leave him as he hails, sword in hand, the castle which he thinks will keep him safe from fear and dread, and marches over a rainbow into Valhalla. This is a drastic change. Wotan's contracts certainly restrict or shut down the movement of life, but an impregnable fortress that towers over the lives of all others is an even more potent symbol of an even stronger determination to keep everything as it is. Wotan's defensive strategy suggests that at some level he knows that something is wrong.

It is Erda who gives voice to Wotan's disquiet, and Wagner makes sure that we and the god listen carefully. Her appearance is great theater. "The stage has darkened again," directs Wagner, and "out of a chasm at the side a bluish ray of light bursts forth"; Erda rises out of the depths, "of noble stature" and cloaked in black hair.[29] The squabbling and anger are stilled, and the nature motif takes shape as Erda's own richly harmonized minor-key theme. Wotan is riveted. So are we; something of tremendous importance is about to happen.

As the music shows, Erda is the voice of nature itself. She speaks as an oracle, and surely she has something that Wotan needs to hear. She herself is happy to recite her credentials. Asked who she is she tells Wotan that she knows past, present, and future, as she is the primordial seer of the eternal world. She is the source of the knowledge that the Norns, her daughters, impart to him every night, but the deep danger in which he finds himself demanded that she speak to him directly.[30]

This is quite a build-up, and we would be justified in expecting an extraordinary revelation. But what Erda tells Wotan sounds, at first, to be

---

28 Williams, *On Opera*, 77.
29 Deathridge translation, 133.
30 *R*, lines 1693–1707.

either unnecessary or pointless. Flee the curse of the Ring, she warns. It is true that the god, with his customarily breezy self-assurance, had made light of Alberich's curse,[31] but it seems bathetic to have an all-knowing being reveal herself just to remind him that Alberich meant what he said, and Erda does not get through to him anyway. Wotan does not understand the power of the curse until he sees Fafner murder his brother,[32] and that takes place after she had left him in "care and fear."

There is more to Erda's warnings than this, though. She cautions Wotan that if he keeps his trophy he dooms himself "to dark destruction without rescue,"[33] and just before vanishing she tells him, "Everything that is—ends." As her motif is inverted, to become what is usually labeled the "Twilight of the Gods" motif, she says, "A dark day dawns for the gods" (the German word is the same for dawn and dusk), and adds, "I advise you, shun the Ring."[34]

Generations of scholars have puzzled over these statements. If Wotan avoids the Ring, why would a dark day dawn for him and his fellow deities? What is it that Erda refers to when she tells Wotan that everything must end? At the end of *Götterdämmerung* the Ring goes back to the Rhinemaidens; why must Valhalla burn?

There are some more-or-less conventional answers to these questions. Warren Darcy puts them this way:

> Erda apprises the god of his own mortality; he, along with everything that lives, is fated to pass away. With only a limited time at his disposal—not all eternity, as he had formerly thought—Wotan can save himself from "irretrievable dark perdition"—from everlasting damnation—only by relinquishing the ring of power and atoning for his past behaviour. This will not spare him physical destruction—which during the course of the tetralogy he learns to accept and ultimately to embrace—but it will afford him spiritual salvation.[35]

Hardly any of this stands up. The Norse gods are mortal and dependent on Freia's golden apples, and Wotan certainly knows this. The word Darcy translates as "perdition" is "Verderben," which generally means destruction or ruin. Wagner is unlikely to have used it to mean damnation, not just on linguistic grounds but because damnation requires a

---

31 *R*, line 1540.
32 *R*, lines 1718, 1766–67.
33 *R*, lines 1689–91.
34 *R*, lines 1710–12.
35 Darcy, *Das Rheingold*, 198–99.

superior authority who can send the gods to hell, and the *Ring* knows no supreme being or creator. All of Darcy's talk about perdition, atonement, and "spiritual salvation," in fact, simply imposes a Christian framework onto Wagner's thoroughly pagan cosmos.

Those puzzles are not so easily solved, and Wagner must bear some of the blame. The character of Erda owes little to Norse mythology, and it is widely assumed that he thought of her in terms of Greek oracles. As he worked and reworked this scene he made her pronouncements more and more oracular and less and less specific. In the prose draft she speaks to all the gods, and she tells them that though *their* end is inevitable, if slow in coming, it would fall upon them suddenly if Wotan does not give up the Ring.[36] She says something similar in the verse draft, where she addresses Wotan directly: a dark day dawns for the gods, whom she calls "dein edles geschlecht" (your noble family/race), but their fate will be shameful if Wotan keeps the Ring. Her focus is not on Wotan's mortality but on the passing of the entire race of gods.

When Wagner set the text to music, though, he cut the reference to the gods as a group, prefaced what was left with "Alles, was ist—endet," and then had Erda simply advise Wotan to shun the Ring. She had already connected possession of the Ring with destruction or a shameful end, and Wagner presumably saw no need to repeat the point, but his compression left some ambiguity between individual and collective calamities.

"Everything that is—ends." Darcy tries to read this both ways, as a warning of Wotan's personal mortality and of "an all-inclusive *Weltuntergang*";[37] he is one of those interpreters who think that the entire universe is wiped out at the end of the cycle.[38] But there is another interpretation which makes a better fit with Wagner's overall thinking as well as his text and stage directions. The combination of the rising Nature motif with the falling theme of the twilight of the gods suggests nothing more than universal mutability. Everything falls and rises again, for the infinite productivity of the real is also infinite destruction. What Erda reminds Wotan, then, is simply the way of all things. The gods' reign and Wotan's order are not exempt. Freia's apples notwithstanding, too, will pass away, to be replaced by something else.

Wotan has assumed that his world would be different. It was supposed to last forever, and he had Valhalla built to make sure that it did.

---

36 "langsam nehet euch ein ende"; Darcy, *Das Rheingold*, 198.
37 Darcy, *Das Rheingold*, 198.
38 Some of the reasons for rejecting this interpretation are found in chapter 9, below.

That was a sign of fear, not confidence; one does not erect a fortress if one has no enemies, and an enemy does show up in the form of Alberich. With the Nibelung, however, Wotan imagines that he has had a stroke of luck. Alberich has inadvertently made it possible for him to have the ultimate weapon, and once he has it he wants to keep it. Ask for anything else, he tells Fafner, but he will not surrender the Ring for anything in the world.[39] And Erda intervenes right after he repeats that insistence "with the most unrelenting resolve."[40]

Wotan thinks that the Ring the key to "peace through strength." He could not be more wrong. It would, instead, mean the end of the very order he is trying to secure. It is true that contractual systems all rest on a monopoly of force, but by common if unspoken consent the legitimate use of violence is limited, confined to the last-resort enforcement of freely assumed obligations. It has been domesticated, subject to discussion and process.

Absolute power, like that inherent in the Ring, is different. It cannot be tamed or constrained by contracts or laws. It is an existential threat when it is exercised outside of such an order, but it would be equally destructive if Wotan were to try to bring it within his system. All pretense of equality and consent would vanish.

Wotan's rule depends on those pretenses, as E. P. Thompson had almost grudgingly argued:

> The essential precondition for the effectiveness of law, in its function as ideology, is that it shall display an independence from gross manipulation and shall seem to be just. It cannot seem to be so without upholding its own logic and criteria of equity; indeed, on occasion, by actually *being* just. And furthermore it is not often the case that a ruling ideology can be dismissed as a mere hypocrisy; even rulers find a need to legitimize their power, to moralize their functions, to feel themselves to be useful and just.[41]

Legalities and the moral validity of contracts would collapse the moment Wotan used the Ring to get his way, and in fact they would collapse even before then, in the first moment of anticipatory obedience, when anyone did any one thing rather than another for fear that the gods might be

---

39 *R*, lines 1672–75.
40 1876 stage direction in the Deathridge translation, 133.
41 E. P. Thompson, *Whigs and Hunters: The Origin of the Black Act* (New York: Pantheon, 1975), 263.

displeased.[42] Wotan's order would henceforth rest on nothing but irresistible force. Alberich's curse is almost beside the point; like most of the "magical" elements in Wagner's plots, it is primarily a way of representing inherent tendencies or relations. Wotan cannot use or even keep the Ring, cursed or not, without destroying his own creation and leading the gods to a shameful end.

The question is what price he is willing to pay—or demand—to maintain his order. There is always a price, and he has been paying it by fighting a constant rear-guard action against the unruly impulsion of natural necessity, endlessly maneuvering, bargaining, and castle-building. To secure that order through arbitrary force, though, would exact a higher price, not just in quantity but in quality. It would replace a tolerably consensual order with "stiff, dogmatic, fettering and domineering might."[43] It is bad enough for Wotan to install himself in Valhalla, "the unnatural height whence [he] fain would guide our Human Nature far below."[44] For him to rely on the Ring is far worse, because that would negate the flawed but nonetheless well-intentioned principles from which he started.

Wotan's renunciation, when it does finally come, is at heart a refusal to pay that price. It is a long time coming, however, and in a sense it comes too late. Wagner told Röckel:

> At the end of "Rhine Gold" when Loge watches the gods enter Walhalla and speaks these fateful words: "They hasten towards their end who imagine themselves so strong in their might," he, in that moment, only gives utterance to our own conviction; for any one who has followed the prelude sympathetically, and not in a hypercritical, cavilling spirit, but abandoning himself to his impressions and feelings, will entirely agree with Loge.[45]

Wagner does not expand on this—it is supposed to be obvious, though it is not—but it is already clear that the end of the gods has been determined. In historians' jargon it is overdetermined. Every order is temporary and every order based on a separation from natural necessity undermines itself.

Worse yet, although Wotan gave up the Ring he still profits from Alberich's crime. Valhalla, as an assertion of power, is not all that different from the Ring—something Wagner had underlined in the interlude that

---

42 Contemporary parallels are unavoidable.
43 *Opera and Drama*, PW II, 196.
44 *Opera and Drama*, PW II, 192.
45 *Letters to August Roeckel*, 104 (January 25–26, 1854), SL 309.

links the first two scenes of the drama, when the Ring motif transforms into the motif for Valhalla—and the Ring was part of its purchase price. The rest came from Alberich's hoard, which would never have existed without the Ring's magic. The castle *is* the gold.

Loge, the *Ring*'s only intellectual, understands this before anyone else. As the drama ends the gods are walking into Valhalla, and Wotan, struck with a "great idea" for managing the Alberich problem, follows them over the rainbow bridge. Loge stays behind, ambivalent. Hearing the lament of the Rhinemaidens, Wotan tells him to silence their taunts, and Loge calls down, "If the gold no longer gleams on you girls, you can sunbathe yourselves happily in the gods' new splendor."[46] And well might the Rhinemaidens bask in the glory of Valhalla; they were the ones who paid for it. Wotan certainly didn't.

---

46 *R*, lines 1871–74, my translation.

7: *Die Walküre:* Reasons of State

WHEN THE CURTAIN rises in *Die Walküre*, we see a primitive house built around a huge ash tree. A storm is dying down and a warrior unlatches the door and stumbles in, wounded and weaponless; Wagner says that "he has the appearance of someone overwrought by excessive struggle; his clothes and the way he looks suggest he is a fugitive."[1] This is Siegmund, the great hero that Wotan has fathered and raised and the key player in the god's "great idea" for snatching the Ring from Fafner and ensuring that Alberich never regains it. His part in Wotan's plotting has all but destroyed him.

A moment later a woman enters from a back room: Sieglinde. Her life, too, has been torn from her thanks to her unasked-for role in Wotan's scheme. Motherless, lost to the rest of her family, forced into a marriage that is little more than legally sanctioned rape, she can barely acknowledge her own existence. When Siegmund asks her name she "wants to give an honest answer, but thinks better of it." She exists in the third person: this house and this woman are Hunding's own, she tells him.[2]

Die Walküre has always been the popular favorite of the *Ring* dramas, but, as Dahlhaus writes, its "overwhelming spell ... emanates less from the whole, for it is no whole, than from individual acts, the first and the third."[3] That spell is even more selective than Dahlhaus suggests; what remain most vividly in memory from the first act, which is often and effectively presented by itself as a concert piece, are the matchless delicacy of its evocation of dawning love and the theatrical grandiosity of its climax, the door's opening to let spring flood into the hall, Siegmund's heroic but tender *Winterstürme*, and his drawing the sword from the tree. Just as with the third act, which is often reduced to the Ride of the Valkyries and Wotan's Farewell, we remember parts and not the whole. We think of it as a love story.

It is that, but the Volsung twins' passionate connection cannot last. For one night, and one night only, they inhabit the different world we make

---

1 Deathridge translation, 153.
2 *W* I, lines 28–29, Deathridge's translation with Wagner's 1876 stage direction. "Weib" can also mean "wife."
3 Dahlhaus, *Richard Wagner's Music Dramas*, 119.

when we fall in love, and the entire course of their lives forms itself into a story that has its inevitable fulfillment in their union. Such bliss rarely if ever lasts; the world and the past push back in—something that figures in *Tristan und Isolde*—and for Siegmund and Sieglinde all the horrors of their lives return in the harsh, cold morning after their night of love.

Watch Act One and Sieglinde's scenes in Act Two, and what one sees and hears is almost-unbearable suffering. Were it not for its compassion and specificity Wagner's portrayal of Sieglinde could have come from a textbook on emotional or psychological abuse, although the *Ring* long predates that concept. She has learned to keep her feelings to herself and even from herself; when she tells Siegmund that he cannot bring misfortune to a house where misfortune dwells, she "is shaken to the depths of her being by her own confession."[4] She lives by the care and cunning of the powerless, controlling her every move and concealing her own plans under a show of submissiveness which is convincing enough to Hunding that he suspects nothing when she deferentially hands him a night-drink laced with drugs.

Freed from his gaze thanks to the drink, and emboldened by the growing love she shares with Siegmund, she fantasizes revenge, repayment for all that she has suffered; she will hunt down all that she had lost and win back everything that she has mourned.[5] The very next morning, though, she is filled with self-loathing, telling Siegmund, "with an expression of wretchedness and horror wound up to a point of extreme intensity and power," that she has been defiled—not by their incestuous union but by her submission to Hunding, "who had possessed her without love."[6] She begs Siegmund to flee from her, "the accursed one," for she can only bring him shame and disgrace. He tries to comfort her, but she raves on as if she has heard nothing, and not even sleep can give her respite. In the terrible climax of Act Two she relives in a dream the raid that left her mother dead and their home in ashes, and she wakes only to see Siegmund die.

All this is fallout from Wotan's plan. So, too, is Siegmund's suffering, and in his case the suffering is deliberate. To regain the Ring, or at least keep it away from Alberich, Wotan needs to create a hero who rebels against his own laws. He therefore raises Siegmund to be brave and friendless, an enemy to all. Siegmund, like any loving son, sees nothing

---

4   *W* I, lines 69–71, Deathridge's translation with Wagner's 1876 stage direction, albeit rearranged.
5   *W* I, lines 385–95.
6   *W* II, line 1146.

wrong in this. He is fiercely proud of his father Wälse and their life together as outlaws. Wotan, though, can always drop his disguise, go back to Valhalla, and have the Valkyries hand him horns of mead. Siegmund is left to fight with or flee from everyone he encounters. He becomes exactly what Wotan wants to breed, and this tutelage condemns him to his life of "grievous suffering." Wotan can acknowledge this, but he regrets nothing. It is a price worth paying if his world-order is to survive, except, of course, that Wotan does not have to pay it, any more than he had to pay for Valhalla. He passes the cost on to the Volsungs, who are essentially collateral damage. If this causes him any pain he expects sympathy for his having to make them suffer.

This may sound unfair, but it is not unduly so. Wotan is not evil or power-hungry so much as he is caught up in the implacable logic of statecraft. This is clear from the long monologue that stands at the center of *Die Walküre* and which Wagner thought was "the most important scene for the evolution of the whole, great four-part drama."[7] It is not a mere rehash of events that we have already seen enacted. It is a self-portrait, something of a narrative apologia and something of a self-indictment, dark thoughts uttered in a dark mood. In it Wotan looks back on early days spent in the pursuit of the pleasures of love and, when those began to pall, in the impulsive hunt for power. He speaks of his contracts with disgust, blaming them on the untrustworthy and unreliable Loge, and of Alberich and the Ring which he filched and then failed to return to the Rhine.

Then comes the first blow. Once Erda tells him that his authority is doomed his "easy-going nature" vanishes. Desperate to know more, Wotan follows her underground, coerces her with "love magic" (a disturbing phrase), obtains the knowledge he demanded, and fathers Brünnhilde to boot. She could not put his fears to rest, though. Alberich remains a threat whether or not he has the Ring, so Wotan decides he needs an army, a Praetorian Guard. He has a plan for this. Rather than maintaining order among humanity he commands the Valkyries to stir up discord and violence, a winnowing-out war of each against all which allows them to identify and harvest the bravest of human warriors. They retrieve the valiant dead and set them to guard Valhalla. Neither Wotan nor Brünnhilde sees any problem with this stratagem, and neither notices that the god himself shares the blame for the brutality that has blighted Sieglinde's

---

7   Quoted in Dahlhaus, *Richard Wagner's Music Dramas*, 122.

life.[8] If that thought did come to them they would likely have conceded, with a tear in the eye, that this, too, was justified by the greater good.

But Wotan realizes soon enough that all the heroes could not protect him if Alberich were to get back the Ring. He can do nothing about this himself. Fafner holds the Ring by virtue of a contract that binds him, too, and he cannot break this without destroying the basis for his authority. He thus needs another cunning plan, and he carefully works out the strategy familiar to everyone who has seen the *Ring*. He will create a free hero to do what he himself cannot.

That plan, though, rests on self-deception, as Fricka mercilessly shows him. Even Siegmund's rebelliousness is his own creation. Wotan cannot make a free person, only a slave, and thus he would be breaking the contract even if he did get somebody else to do the deed. In the words of a Law Latin tag, *qui facit per alium facit per se*: he who acts through another acts himself. Wotan is powerless when it really counts and he cannot tolerate his frustration. He had taken pleasure in winning the world and striking the contracts that secured his rulership, but the game is no longer worth playing, and in fact it is no longer winnable. Alberich has fathered his own son and cat's-paw, Hagen, and Erda has warned him that this is what will bring the gods' rule to an end, but Wotan has run out of plans. Despondent, he tells Brünnhilde that he desires nothing more than "the End"—not the end of everything, but the end of his rule as king of the gods and the end of the gods' authority.[9] Alberich can take over and do his worst. For the moment, at least, Wotan is beyond caring.

This long monologue is not without its critics; even some of the "music drama's most fervent adherents" have thought that it "hangs fire."[10] Its text, though, is an exemplary fusion of self-revelation and political analysis, developed, as in *Das Rheingold*, through the coexistence of the psychological and the mythic. Wotan is tormented by his lack of freedom, and in the same words lays bare the mythic context of his increasingly fragile reign and the political logic that led him into his tragic impasse. The personal narrative is thus structured around a series of political acts.

---

8   *W* II, lines 975–90. This strife is sometimes erroneously blamed on Alberich's curse.

9   Contrary to some interpretations, *das Ende* is not the end of the world; otherwise there would be no Alberich and nothing for him to rule. In his last speech on the subject, in the third act of *Siegfried*, Wotan similarly tells Erda that he will leave the world to his grandson as his inheritance. This, too, presupposes that the world will continue on its course.

10   Dahlhaus, *Richard Wagner's Music Dramas*, 122.

In December 1871, when he was nearly finished with the score of *Götterdämmerung*, Wagner wrote that his treatment of his mythic material "will become plain enough to anybody who will honour the second section, in particular, of my lengthy treatise on 'Opera and Drama' with a serious inspection."[11] That section is particularly helpful in interpreting *Die Walküre*. It is not quite what most scholarship would lead readers to expect, however. Though Wagner had practical musical-dramatic reasons for the scale of the *Ring* cycle, the trilogies of Athenian tragedy had offered him a model for his structure and for the half-in, half-out character of the "preliminary evening," *Das Rheingold*, which has often been compared to the satyr plays that accompanied tragic works,[12] and Wagner's ambition is often seen in terms of his veneration of Aeschylus. Where content is concerned, though, neither the *Oresteia* nor an erroneous "reconstruction" of a Prometheus trilogy is as relevant as Sophocles' first two Theban plays are.[13] The progression of Wotan's monologue, for example, parallels the philosophical history of the state that Wagner had developed from a reading of those plays, a history which traces, as Borchmeyer says, a relentless decline "from utilitarianism and abstract custom to moral indifference."[14] In families and small communities human lives had been shaped by the "purely human," "a letting-arise from the root itself."[15] Narrow and restrictive as those might be, they were still shaped by shared experience. As time passed, however, even the limited flexibility and openness of those communities gave way to a fixed and reliable order grounded in habit or inertia. Wagner, somewhat anachronistically, saw this as the birth of bourgeois society, where the maintenance of peace and quiet, legal order, and property relations is deemed "the highest political wisdom."[16] This, of course, is hard to distinguish from the contract-state over which Wotan presides.

To secure that order, though, the state suppressed "the holiest and most instinctive social feelings,"[17] the expression of nature's ceaseless

---

11   Richard Wagner, "Epilogue to the "Nibelung's Ring," *PW* III, 257.

12   See, generally, David Sansone, "Wagner, Droysen and the Greek Satyr-Play," *Antike und Abendland* 61, no. 1 (2015): 1–9. Wagner tended to refer to the *Ring* as a trilogy.

13   There is an extensive discussion of this in Jason Geary, "Greek Tragedy and Myth," in *The Cambridge Companion to Wagner's "Der Ring des Nibelungen,"* esp. 64–69.

14   Borchmeyer, *Richard Wagner: Theory and Theatre*, 294.

15   *Opera and Drama, PW* II, 193.

16   *Opera and Drama, PW* II, 188.

17   *Opera and Drama, PW* II, 184.

and all-pervasive creativity. As we have seen, in such an order the true life of humanity lies concealed within the blank faces of interchangeable but nominally separate individuals, breaking out every now and then "in tones of yearning and finally of revolt."[18] Its stability is a facade. Under the surface every state exists "in perpetual change, as constantly incipient variations of an inexecutable theme—a violent, but yet an ever interrupted and contested footing."[19] To shore up that facade is a doomed struggle. "Since the establishment of the political State, no single step has been taken in history but, let it be directed with never so deliberate aim to that State's consolidation, has led towards its downfall."[20]

That is what Wotan is beginning to discover. What had once been a whirl of inspired improvisations has become a nightmare. Every step he takes now only makes his problems worse. The earth falls into bloody chaos, he fails to create a free hero, and his plan itself not only creates more human misery, it places him in a position in which, for perfectly justifiable reasons of state, he has to ensure the death of his own son. Wagner may well have been thinking of this when he wrote, angrily, that the Thebans would have been content if Oedipus's father had managed to murder his son to protect himself, because "Quiet and Order were at any rate more worth considering than the most natural of human sentiments, which bids a father sacrifice himself to his children, not them to *him*."[21]

The parallels are not exact, perhaps, but the opposition between the maintenance of "quiet and order" and the surging life of natural human sentiments runs through the *Ring* cycle and through *Die Walküre* in particular. This may sound close to or identical with the conventional interpretation that the *Ring* is about power versus love, but it is, in fact, something quite different. It has nothing to do with emotions. Wotan may be power-mad, but he does not need to be so flawed to act as he does, and we would not care so much about him if he were. He simply needs to be committed to maintaining a specific world order so firmly that everything and everyone else must be sacrificed for its survival.

This is worse than a crime. It is a mistake. The historical argument of *Opera and Drama* is that, in the long term, a battle like Wotan's can never be won. The *Ring* cycle makes much the same argument, but it is a drama, not a history, and it centers on the Ring because Alberich's

---

18 See chapter 6, above.
19 *Opera and Drama*, *PW* II, 191–92.
20 *Opera and Drama*, *PW* II, 191–92. All of this is clearly foreshadowed in the notes for *Jesus of Nazareth*, cited above.
21 *Opera and Drama*, *PW* II, 188.

theft of the gold and forging of the Ring speeds up that process. It puts Wotan's order under such intense pressure that it is tested to the breaking point. The pressure does, ultimately, break it. The gods' world comes to an end, as Erda had warned him it would.

The best Wotan could do, she had added, would be to keep that end from becoming shameful. He does indeed avoid that fate, but he fails to resolve the problem of Alberich's Ring. He does not have to be the character who does that, however; the limits of his world are not the limits of the world itself. The Ring does not need to remain a permanent threat. It is dealt with, but not by some superior plan or a more responsive political structure. The process starts unexpectedly, with a spontaneous act by Wotan's and Erda's daughter. Brünnhilde does not act with this or any other end in mind, but she will open the way to the genuinely necessary resolution of the drama and of both of its narratives. She inches her way towards a world open to the life of the real.

Brünnhilde's actions are clear enough. She disobeys Wotan's explicit command to fight on behalf of Hunding. She takes Siegmund's side instead, and when he falls she lifts the pregnant Sieglinde onto her horse and flees her father's fury. The more difficult question is why she does these things. Cooke insists that she has been won over by Siegmund's refusal to go to Valhalla, since Sieglinde cannot accompany him: "In the long struggle between power and love ... love has always—despite its apparent triumph in Act 1 of *The Valkyrie*—been totally on the losing side; but now that it has its back to the wall, and seems certain to be extinguished, it makes a tremendous come-back, through Siegmund's love-motivated act of rebellion against the highest manifestation of power."[22] Brünnhilde stops fighting for power and starts fighting for love.

Well, maybe. Or maybe not. "Power" and "love" have no agency, and they do not flit around in the *Ring* like the good and bad angels perched on the shoulders of a cartoon character. Siegmund's "act of rebellion" is a polite and wholly respectful decision to decline a thoughtful and generous offer, and Brünnhilde's first response is to save Sieglinde and leave Siegmund to his fate.

These are quibbles, though, compared with another weakness in the conventional power-love interpretation: it narrows the focus of the cycle. In Cooke's interpretation, which is not the least sophisticated presentation of this view, Wagner's "vision of a possible future change in human nature is largely acted out in the hearts of one or two individuals. The emphasis progressively shifts from society to the individual, from the

---

22 Cooke, *I Saw the World End*, 336–37.

outer to the inner, so as to concentrate on imagined new types of humanity, exemplifying the way in which the change may come about."[23]

This reduces the *Ring* to a fifteen-hour sermon on something Jimi Hendrix could say in a sentence: "When the power of love overcomes the love of power the world will know peace." Wagner was a better philosopher than Hendrix, though, and he would have seen at once where Cooke had gone wrong. The oppositions Cooke takes for granted, between society and the individual and between the outer and the inner, have come about through the separation of self-conscious humanity from the real and the natural. They are precisely what humanity needs to overcome. In this view Wagner was entirely in accord with classical German philosophy and the Jena Romantics. He agreed with them, and with Marx, in seeing that no order based on the separation of self and world could be transformed without doing away with that separation. Self and world must be brought together and changed together.

It is not even necessary to know Wagner's prose works to recognize this, or to see that he would reject the idea that social change could come about through individual self-transformation. The overall course of the *Ring* casts cold water on the naïve faith that the bliss and clarity of egoless love is sufficient in itself or that one only need to "become the change one wants to see in the world."[24] Brünnhilde and Siegfried are genuinely transformed by their passion, but from the moment they step into the world of the Gibichungs they are defenseless. Wagner said sometimes that the *Ring* was about the fate of the revolution, and at other times that it was about the fate of the world or one particular world; he never made up his mind. Choose any one of the three: the political and social questions are still essential.

Die Walküre contains none of the specific contemporary references that are so obvious in *Das Rheingold*, but this does not mean that Wagner had abandoned the "broad social interpretation" that Cooke sees in the first of the dramas. Brünnhilde's defiance of her father is a political act. It is not a calculated, rational move; she acts spontaneously, without ego or any form of self-regard, not for a moment thinking of the consequences to herself or anyone else. It is nonetheless inconsistent with the order that Wotan strives to maintain. At the same time, however, it is a moment of illumination and indeed of love. Brünnhilde both makes and becomes the change, and her act has direct political ramifications, because she makes it possible for Wotan to change as well.

---

23 Cooke, *I Saw the World End*, 275.
24 The attribution of this adage to Gandhi is incorrect.

Here, too, the second part of *Opera and Drama* shows Wagner's intentions, primarily in his depiction of Antigone. Brünnhilde has clearly been modeled on Sophocles' heroine, whose brother, killed in a plausibly justifiable assault on the city, has been declared an outlaw and must be left unburied. Antigone goes to her death because she defies the law of Thebes and performs his funeral rights. This would seem to present the most explicit of oppositions between power and love, and in Wagner's time Antigone's love for her brother was central to her appeal as a character. Sisterliness, as George Steiner writes, was a pervasive ideal in nineteenth-century Europe, creator after creator testifying to "the persuasion that the love between brother and sister is at once the heart's heart and the transcendence of the erotic."[25] And does not Brünnhilde throw away her divinity to stand up for Siegmund, who is in fact her half-brother?

She does not do that consciously. The text of *Die Walküre* never mentions this relationship. Surprisingly, though, this does not distance Brünnhilde from her Greek model. It brings them closer together, because Wagner, unlike the rest of his contemporaries, discounted family relations entirely in his analysis. It was "the flower of Love" that blossomed in Antigone, but this "was not the love of sex, not love of child to parent, not love of sister for her brother." It was "pure Human-love," which spoke with the voice of necessity:

> Antigone's love was *fully conscious*. She knew, what she was doing,— but she also knew that do it she must, that she had no choice but to act according to love's Necessity; she knew, that she had to listen to this unconscious, strenuous necessity of *self-annihilation in the cause of sympathy*; and in this consciousness of the Unconscious she was alike the perfect Human Being, the embodiment of Love in its highest fill and potence.[26]

And her self-sacrifice led, through the suicide of the ruler's son, to the end of the Theban state, which was thus "annulled" by "the love-curse of Antigone."[27]

Wagner never used terms carefully and unambiguously, as philosophers are supposed to do, and when he wrote dramatic works he let his characters use them even more loosely. Wotan's notion of love, for example, can sound worryingly close to sexual harassment or even sexual extortion—who can say no to the king of the gods? In his prose writings,

---

25 Steiner, *Antigones*, 12.
26 *Opera and Drama*, PW II, 189.
27 *Opera and Drama*, PW II, 189.

too, Wagner employs "love" in so many different contexts that it cannot have just one clear definition. It operates more like a pointer to a family of phenomena, and Antigone's "pure Human-love" hardly resembles any more familiar kind of love. Like the deepest love between partners, however, it is fundamentally ethical in nature. It is a condition of pure, egoless acceptance, a willingness to set aside one's own individual wants and needs to become a pure presentation of reality. That is where Antigone takes her stand. Emptying herself of herself, rising above her fear of death, she becomes its voice and tool, speaking for everything that the State has rejected and repressed: the "purely human." Antigone is radically free. She does not act out of individual or familial interests but out of a vast, impersonal love, the love that moves the sun and other stars, with the freedom that Kant saw as obedience to the moral law and that Fichte saw as true blessedness.

There is no real need to ponder Brünnhilde's motives for taking the side of the twins, for they are essentially the same. "Antigone knew nothing of politics; —she loved," Wagner wrote in *Opera and Drama*,[28] and a few years later he wrote to Röckel, "Where Wotan clung to schemes, [Brünnhilde] could only—love."[29] The verbal echoes suggest the same kind of all-encompassing acceptance and compassion. Brünnhilde, too, becomes a votary of the moral law. She does not throw her lot in with Siegmund because he and Sieglinde love each other; only after Siegmund prepares to kill his sister and their unborn child does she decide to fight on his side. In Act Three she tells Wotan that she had been acting out of the love for Siegmund which he had taught her to feel,[30] but everything that she had said before this had implied no favoritism or family pride. Face to face with Siegmund's deep pain she felt awed and ashamed, she had told Wotan, and she could think of nothing but how to serve him. Nothing else mattered, not even her fear of Wotan's terrifying wrath.

Something else mattered to Wotan, and he had expected it to matter to Brünnhilde, too. Plunged back into the same darkness that had haunted his monologue, he reminds her that he has had to stem the love in his heart because of his love for the world—the greater good, clearly, not any selfish love of power.[31] (Since he is trying to win her sympathy he could not mean this in any other way.) But she ignores his argument.

28   *Opera and Drama*, *PW* II, 189.
29   *Letters to August Roeckel*, 105 (January 25–26, 1854), *SL* 309. The parallels are the same in the original German.
30   *W* III, lines 2201–2.
31   *W* III, lines 2217–19.

From Wotan's perspective Siegmund had to die so that "the world," his world, could survive. This is a utilitarian, reason-of-state argument and it no longer made any sense to her. She had seen through to the dark side of Wotan's noble dream. Its price was no longer distant, no longer an abstraction. She had seen that price for herself, and she would not ask anyone to pay it.

Wotan does not overreact in punishing her so severely, then. Her refusal is just as much a political act as a presidential guard's laying down arms; she has indeed excluded herself from the company of the gods. That betrayal is more bitter because Wotan himself is torn. He protests repeatedly that he, too, loved Siegmund, and even though he seems to focus on his own distress, rather than on the distress that he imposes on others, there is no reason to doubt the genuineness of his emotion. The intensity of that conflict may account for the "vehemence" with which he responds to Brünnhilde's mention of the Volsungs—"Shut up about them!"—and of Sieglinde's unborn child—"Don't try to get me to protect the woman or the fruit of her womb!"[32]

And yet he relents. He does not take back his punishment, and in fact he is right in telling Brünnhilde that she herself had chosen it. She could never return to the company of the other Valkyries. In his rage and disappointment he had thought, at first, of degrading her, making her the slave of the first man that came along. She pleads for mercy, but Wotan stands firm until she makes one last, desperate request: that she be surrounded by fire so that only the most fearless, freest hero can wake her. This is the real turning point of the Wotan narrative.

We might think that Brünnhilde has finally worn her father down, that she is so clearly noble in her being and intentions that his love for her overcomes all else. Wotan, though, has long been able to deny himself the luxury of feelings. Brünnhilde cannot win him over to the importance of love or show him the emptiness of the pursuit of power. He is aware of all that, but he has been in no position to act on that knowledge. What counts is political necessity, and as a ruler he cannot allow himself to be distracted. He has a world to run.

What Brünnhilde does is alter that world, and Wotan could not have let himself hear her if she had not done that. "You ask for too much," he says at first. Ever since she had told him about Sieglinde's pregnancy, though, the Siegfried motif has been weaving in and out of the score, and Wotan finally senses what the orchestra knows. He has failed to create a hero, but as Brünnhilde throws her arms around his knees and

---

32   *W* III, lines 2286–2300, my translation. Wagner's 1876 stage direction.

repeats her plea he understands, at last, that one is coming anyway, one who is freer than he is himself, and this one fact makes everything different. He will not mention Siegfried by name, but his vocal line is one of Siegfried's motifs.

The personal and political are so intertwined here that there can be no question of precedence. Wotan's love for his daughter allows him to see that Alberich and Hagen do not need to triumph, and knowing that fact frees him to listen to his love. And it is love, in the fullest sense in which Wagner uses the word. Wotan will let the world take care of itself, which is an act of trust as much as it is one of renunciation.

Wotan had told himself that his own world order, as flawed and cruel as it had become, was still preferable to anything that might replace it; whatever he said in his second-act monologue, he was not ready to let the world fall into Alberich's hands. Now, for the first time, he could see that this was not the only possibility, and that something better could follow the end of what he had built. He lets slip the crushing responsibility of rulership, and with that act he finds that he can look at his child with pride, love, and even gratitude. She herself is the free person he could not create. By rebelling against him she has acted out of the highest morality, which is a free act in its deepest sense, and in saving Sieglinde and her child she had freed him from the world's weight. Brünnhilde, like Sieglinde, carries the future within herself, and Wotan knows now that he must step aside so she can make that future on her own. He kisses her divinity away and lays her gently on the ground, calls up Loge's magic fire, and bars the way through the flames to anyone who fears the tip of his spear—to anyone but Siegfried. These are the last things he accomplishes as king of the gods. He walks slowly away from his sleeping daughter. He walks away from Valhalla, too.

8. *Siegfried:* Stasis and Movement

WAGNER WAS WORKING on the score of Act Two of *Siegfried* when he started having second thoughts. He had begun *Das Rheingold* in 1853, but now, in 1857, he was ready to give up his "headstrong design of completing the *Nibelungen*."[1] He put *Siegfried* aside, picked it up again to complete the second act, and then stopped work on it altogether. He could see no way for the *Ring* to be produced, and so he decided to write something more commercially viable, a drama on a smaller scale that would be within the capacities of lesser opera houses.

The result was *Tristan und Isolde*, which does have a small cast but which grew to be so demanding and avant-garde that after seventy rehearsals the Vienna Court Opera, one of the greatest of European theaters, gave up trying to mount the premiere. His next project was *Die Meistersinger*, the longest piece in the operatic repertory, which he was working on when, in 1864, Ludwig II was crowned king of Bavaria. The young king was obsessed with Wagner, and he sent his idol an emissary—whom Wagner turned away at first, thinking he was a hoaxer—and promised to settle the composer's debts and see to the production of all of his works, the *Ring* included. By the time Wagner had finished *Die Meistersinger* and returned to the cycle eleven years had passed, but everything went well, and at the end of February 1869 he could write to his wife and King Ludwig that *"Siegfried* is divine. It is my greatest work!"[2] He expected that it would become the most popular drama in the cycle.

That never happened. *Die Walküre* is usually the audience favorite and many musicians and scholars prefer *Götterdämmerung*.[3] *Siegfried* is often the least liked of the four, in fact. Too many male voices, people say; too much fairy tale and not enough human drama. There is near universal admiration for the Forest Murmurs and other scene painting, but the highest praise for the piece is often that it is a kind of colorful or pleasurable interlude, the "scherzo of the cycle," a breathing space

---

1   Letter to Franz Liszt, June 28, 1857, *SL* 370.
2   February 23–24, 1857, *SL* 739.
3   Theodor Adorno and Edward Said are exceptions; both preferred *Siegfried*.

between Wotan's wrenching farewell and the scheming and calamities of *Götterdämmerung*.

Wagner had a point, however. *Siegfried* is anything but an interlude. It is the central drama of the *Ring* cycle; *Rheingold* is no more than a prelude, and Wagner always thought of the whole as a trilogy. Its centrality is not just formal, either. It brings us to the high point in the *Ring* in both personal and political terms, catching us up in a moment of brilliant promise that makes the betrayals and deaths of the last drama all the more painful.

Wagner's pride in the work makes sense from a compositional and dramatic perspective, too. In no other work had he surpassed its fusion of form and content, which unite an emotionally cogent story with the cycle's social and philosophical themes. To see and hear it with those themes in mind helps us see why Wagner would value it even over the masterpieces that he had written in the interim.

It is not without problems. The first and most obvious is the title character. Siegfried never shows much self-awareness or emotional depth, and in the first act, especially, he is gratuitously nasty to Mime, threatening him repeatedly, obsessively proclaiming his loathing in viciously physical terms, and mocking his looks, posture, and patterns of speech. Wagner gushed over his "godlike simplicity," but we are more likely to see him as a playground bully or a rebellious teenager.

Siegfried *is* a teenager, though, and his flamboyant hatred of Mime is only slightly more extreme than what we might expect of any lonely, confused, and impulsive child confronting a foster father whose parental advice is filled with both lies and self-justification. The role can be taken only by a tenor of heroic abilities, however, and as a result we have a grown man, with the voice of an adult, impersonating an adolescent. The attempt has to fail. Siegfried comes across as a man-child, and his emotional volatility and immaturity appear to be character defects rather than the forgivable symptoms of a difficult youth. This is a dilemma which could possibly have been minimized had Siegfried been a trouser role; a soprano might have been better able to impersonate Wagner's prodigious stripling. That is not what Wagner chose, however, and it is not hard to imagine how he would have reacted had anybody been foolhardy enough to make such a suggestion. We are stuck with a tenor.

Mime, too, can be hard to deal with. In Norse and Germanic lore dwarfs were thought of as skilled craftspeople and fearsome warriors. They were not generally ugly and were not even necessarily short. Wagner leaves their height unclear in the *Ring*, which perhaps absolves him of creating a stereotype of little people, but he leaves no doubt that they are supposed to be unattractive; both Mime and his brother Alberich are likened to toads. But that is not the real problem. Ever since Mahler, if not before, Mime has been seen as an antisemitic stereotype—it is one that Mahler applied to himself—and the association has been so widely accepted that a recent paper refers to him as "the Jewish dwarf of Wagner's *Ring* Cycle," as if this were obvious.[4]

That goes too far. Mime is not Jewish. There are no Jews in the *Ring*'s universe, and no Christians either. All the same, Mime's "shuffling and shambling," his "weak-kneed and nodding" posture and his "blinking" eyes—in Siegfried's words—are all too reminiscent of Wagner's caricatures of Jews, and his vocal line is said to echo Wagner's terminally unsympathetic impression of the singing in traditional synagogues. Bad enough as this is, Mime's eventual death at Siegfried's hands looks like the justifiable killing of a Jewish villain by an Aryan blond beast, and that is even worse.

How this plays out in performance is another matter. Wagner generally sees through the eyes of all of his characters, even the unattractive ones, and he allows Siegfried and Mime alike to have good reasons for what they do. The plot makes it inevitable that one will kill the other; hero and dwarf both plausibly think that they are acting in self-defense. It is hard to see this as the justifiable extermination of an inhuman alien. Some viewers may bring Nazi associations to Mime's death, but those are not implicit in the text or music.

The odor of antisemitic intentions still clings to Mime, but there is no reason for it to taint a performance of *Siegfried*. Jews, as a whole, do not resemble Wagner's stereotype any more than they resemble Fagin or the Merchant of Venice. I am a Jew myself, and I have never come across a fellow Jew who shuffled, shambled, nodded, and blinked more than anyone else, or who could be described as weak-kneed. Some Jews are like that, I suppose, but so are some Christians and some Tibetan Buddhists. When I see a character who has those traits I have no reason to think of Judaism. I have also spent my share of Saturday mornings in synagogues, both Orthodox and Conservative, and nobody in any of them sounded like Mime.

Mime would look like a Jew only to somebody who thinks that such a caricature is accurate. The responsibility for that falls on the spectator. Viewers less likely to fall into that trap might instead think of Mime as an example of certain disturbing nineteenth-century attitudes towards Jews. This may be an accurate assessment, but anyone who engages in such

---

4   Genevieve Robyn Arkle, "Gustav Mahler and the Crisis of Jewish Masculinity," *19th-Century Music* 47, no. 3 (2024): 157–75.

analysis while watching is either insensitive to the drama or has the misfortune to be attending an inept performance. For *Siegfried* works very well in the theater.

It is indeed a fairy tale, at least up to the end of the second act, and like all good fairy tales it takes place in its own timeless somewhere-else, in a once-upon-a-time kingdom or "a long time ago in a galaxy far, far away." But Wagner does something more interesting than set his tale in a world where time stands still. He dramatizes that immobility and gives it philosophical weight. Reality is movement and is manifest in change, so stasis is an illegitimate confinement or repression of what truly exists. It must always be overcome. That is the overarching structure of the drama. The movement of the *Ring* has come to a halt, and it takes a hero to get it moving again.

This arises, in fact, out of a twofold impasse. At the end of *Die Walküre* Wotan had taken away Brünnhilde's divinity and cast her into a magical sleep. Until she is awakened she cannot move the story forward, and Siegfried will have to be born and grow to manhood before that can happen. Her branch of the drama has been put on hold, and the music tells us as much; as the curtain falls on the sleeping Valkyrie the Fate motif is suspended, as Cooke says. Instead of "moving mysteriously from one key to another" it "is held fixed in the key in which the opera ends."[5]

The plotting and machinations about the Ring itself have also been paused. We need to remember that the Ring is a bit like the McGuffin in a Hitchcock movie; aside from Alberich and Mime, nobody really wants it.[6] Within the Wotan narrative, especially, what drives the action is not so much the god's desire for power as the fear that someone else might have it. Fafner, who wanted Freia not for herself but to deprive the gods of the golden apples, holds the Ring for the same reason—to keep it out of the gods' hands—but he has inadvertently done them a favor. Wotan surely remembers both the curse and Erda's warning in *Das Rheingold*, and though he is always tempted by its power he can see that his own ends are secure as long as Fafner, who terrifies Alberich, keeps the Ring sitting uselessly on his pile of treasure. He also knows that a more permanent solution is possible. Wotan is not at the point of abdication, but he is coming to terms with Brünnhilde's rebellion, and with Siegfried's birth he has a reasonable hope that the twilight of the gods will not be followed by the endless night of Alberich's tyranny. He can wait until his grandson grows up.

---

5 Deryck Cooke, *An Introduction to Wagner's "Der Ring des Nibelungen"* (Decca Records insert), 24.
6 Wotan tells Alberich this, *S* II, lines 1267–70.

Both of the *Ring*'s narratives are in suspended animation. Berger writes: "The first act of Siegfried ... is permeated by the image of going nowhere, of incessant, obsessive turning in circles."[7] We also hear this in the dark and marvelously low-voiced prelude to Act Two of *Siegfried*, with all movement drained away from the opening fragment of the giants' motif, and see it in the scene immediately after that, between Alberich and the Wanderer. Both are at loose ends, waiting to see what will happen. Time has stopped.

This creates the fairy tale world of *Siegfried*, but it also clears the narrative space which allows Wotan to recast himself as the Wanderer. We need not read Schopenhauerian renunciation into his character; while he is increasingly willing to let humanity take over, he is not ready to die and he does not seem to go about in deepest gloom. He can relax and wander, offering help, advice, and comfort to his hosts, perhaps enjoying the company of female humans, and meddling now and then when the impulse strikes him. He is at home among humanity, as he was in the years between the first two dramas, and one might even imagine him taking pleasure in his lack of responsibility.

It can and does get others into trouble, however; Wotan's deadly riddling game with Mime leads directly to the dwarf's death. In every version of his story Wagner had Siegfried killing him, and always because Mime wanted him dead, but in the final version of the *Ring* Mime only starts plotting to kill Siegfried after the Wanderer tells him that he will die at the hands of one who does not know fear. (His panic makes no dramatic sense if he had been planning murder all along.) Mime knows exactly whom the Wanderer is talking about. He assumes that he will be safe if he can only teach Siegfried the meaning of fear, so he tries that first, but as a back-up plan he needs his poison.

Mime fails, of course, but not before he gets Siegfried to kill Fafner. This is the first decisive act in the fairy-tale story. It is also the first step away from that story, though, because everything in *Siegfried* moves naturally and relentlessly towards the shattering of both logjams and the end of the fairy-tale interlude. Siegfried gets the Ring, though he does not know what to do with it, and Act Three ends with Brünnhilde's awakening and her union with Siegfried, through which the two of them become a "complete human being."[8] Everyone and everything has changed utterly.

And it is change, activity, the unfettered creativity of the real, that works through the drama and brings it to its ecstatic close. Siegfried

---

7   Berger, *Beyond Reason*, 119.
8   *Letters to August Roeckel*, 98 (January 25–26, 1854), SL 307.

himself is nothing but action. This makes him a difficult character to identify with, but it is surely what Wagner wanted. He told Röckel that his hero was not "wholly unconscious," but that, for him as an ideal type, "all consciousness must find expression in present life and action."[9] Siegfried wants nothing for himself and accepts things just as they are. His fearlessness lies in that, not his strength, so it is as much ethical as it is physical.

He was different in the 1848 versions of the narrative, where his first act after forging his sword had been to avenge his father's death on Hunding's relatives. Only after that did he set out to kill the dragon. Wagner could include this incident in *Siegfrieds Tod* because it was narrated, not shown, but once he decided to write *Der junge Siegfried* it had to go. It could hardly be represented on stage. This left very little to justify Siegfried's fame as the world's greatest hero, but it also made him look less bloodthirsty, and it avoided suggesting some unnecessary plot complications. Most crucially for the themes of the entire cycle, it eliminated Siegfried's one act as a specific individual, the one deed which spoke of his own history and character.

That revision also left Siegfried with virtually no motivation to do anything on his own. Someone else has to direct him and show him where to turn his energies. He is not the hero of the drama for his outstanding personal qualities; he really has none. His heroism lies in his spontaneity, his effortless personification of nature's activity. In Act One he is not much more than a bumptious boy, and an annoying one at that, but through the course of Act Two he becomes, step by step, the pure presentation of natural necessity, the Real come to life.[10] He finds himself in predawn twilight, alone in the forest and close to Fafner's cave, and his thoughts turn towards his mother. He is overwhelmed with longing, and he does not know where to go or what to do. He feels, as well, how close he is to understanding the significance of the life all around him. He is not yet ready for that knowledge; he makes a pipe from a reed but comically fails to converse with the Woodbird. Once he kills Fafner and tastes his blood, though, he finds that nature itself will guide him. The Woodbird now speaks to him in words that he understands.

Through the midday sun the bird leads him to the treasure and tells him to take the Ring and the Tarnhelm. He then warns Siegfried of Mime's plans, though this is hardly necessary; Siegfried can hear the reality

---

9   *Letters to August Roeckel*, 102 (January 25–26, 1854), *SL* 309.
10 See *A Communication to My Friends*, *PW* I, 375.

of Mime's murderous intentions instead of the lies that Mime speaks.[11] Finally, and most importantly for both Siegfried and the *Ring* as a whole, the Woodbird tells him about the glorious bride who awaits him and leads him towards the flames of Brünnhilde's rock. Siegfried rushes upwards to the most brilliant and ebullient music we have heard so far.

The fairy tale ends here. At the very least, the clocks that have stopped at the end of *Die Walküre* have started again. The Ring is no longer safely tucked away in Fafner's cave and Brünnhilde is on the verge of awakening. Things have become serious, and Wotan is tempted back into his old role. He can no longer let things be. He must be king of the gods once more. He calls up Erda, desperate for guidance, only to find that she is as lost in this new-dawning world as he is. One thing she knows: Wotan is not what he claims to be. Stung by her bitterness, Wotan retorts that she herself is not what she thinks she is.[12]

All this finds expression in the music. The tumultuous prelude to Act Three has far more movement and motivic density than the other preludes had. It was at this point, of course, that Wagner had picked up the composition of the *Ring* after his long hiatus. With *Tristan* and *Meistersinger* behind him his harmonic language had become more subtle and adventurous and he was better able to develop and interweave his thematic material. Intuitively or not, he had found the perfect point at which to lay the score aside. His earlier style was well suited to the fable-like action of the first two acts, but the higher stakes and the interpersonal drama of the last act demanded something richer, and this makes the transition between the Wagner of 1857 and that of 1869 seem natural and even necessary.

Wotan, though, is caught between past and future. He tells Erda that since Siegfried has come into his own he no longer fears that Alberich will prevail, and he will leave the world to his grandson as an inheritance. Not only that, it is not Siegfried but Brünnhilde, their daughter, who will carry out the act that will redeem the world.[13] She will indeed do that, at the very end of *Götterdämmerung*, but she must undergo terrible betrayals and suffering before she knows what that deed must be, and that is a wisdom only she can learn.

For all his paternal and grandfatherly intentions, though, Wotan cannot keep himself from one final assertion of power, "contrary to his high

---

11   The Woodbird is not identified as female, and Wagner wanted the part to be sung by a boy.
12   *S* III, lines 2016–111.
13   *S* III, lines 2127–46.

resolve," Wagner told Röckel. In "a stirring of his ancient pride, brought about by his jealousy for Brünnhilde,"[14] he blocks Siegfried's way up to her rock. This is an almost comical failure; Siegfried can see nothing but a foolish old man and, armed with his newly forged sword, he slices Wotan's spear in two. With it go all the contracts on which the god's authority had rested. Wotan vanishes into darkness as Siegfried climbs towards the light.

Wotan's failed gambit is another of the turning points of the *Ring*. It is where he accepts, at last, that his reign has ended, closing off his own narrative. It also marks the end of one world and opens the space for a new one. As we have seen, Wotan is "the actual sum of the Intelligence of the Present," and though we, like Wotan, long for the humanity of the future, none of us can fashion it; the future must make itself "by means of our annihilation." We need to stop meddling in the future, to surrender our power over what is to come, and that is what happens in this very scene. Wotan's "annihilation" is, in essence, the recognition and acceptance of his own irrelevance, a process which had begun when his favorite daughter rebelled against him and which culminates when his grandson shatters the instrument of his power and strides past him.

Wotan may have imagined a quiet transfer of authority, Siegfried taking over his kingship, but Siegfried is not interested in such an inheritance. He does not want the task of holding together a world that Wotan and Alberich had cut off from its foundations. He wants to do no more than what nature demands of him, and that is what brings him to Brünnhilde and to the long scene that closes the drama.

That scene is more complex than it is often seen to be. Siegfried is easy to lead and to lead astray, which is what precipitates the catastrophes that end the *Ring*, but he is also without fear, and since fear and love stand in opposition his foolishness here is wisdom—a wisdom which terrifies his bride-to-be. The final scene is no mere love duet. It brings together many of the fundamental ideas in Wagner's philosophy and its oppositions between movement and stasis, infinitude and finitude, and trust and fear. These are dramatized, not just discussed, in a slow drawing together of the heroes of the cycle that works through its overarching themes in the most intimate and personal of terms.

Brünnhilde tells Siegfried that she has always loved him, but it is clear that what she had loved was an image, a static idea which posed no threat to her own picture of her self.[15] As soon as her first delight fades she begins to retreat from the real flesh-and-blood Siegfried and take shelter

---

14 *Letters to August Roeckel*, 101 (January 25–26, 1854), SL 308.
15 *S* III, lines 2475–94.

in the relics of her past, holding on to a narcissistic memory of a literally armored security. Her shield and helmet no longer protect her, she laments. Siegfried, who has recovered almost instantly from the fear he felt upon kissing her awake, responds that she herself has wounded his head and heart, which she can do because he has come without helmet or shield. Brünnhilde sees "with increasing sadness" the armor that he had cut away from her sleeping body, and Siegfried tells her that he braved the fire without any armor. In the face of his passion her sight is clouded with darkness, she says, and she feels surrounded by night and terror. Siegfried answers that night encloses eyes that are bound; if she rises from that darkness she would see that the day is bright with sunshine.

Once more begging him to leave her rather than destroy her with his love, Brünnhilde asks Siegfried if he has ever seen his image in the water. If you stir up waves in the stream, she reminds him, the image vanishes in the billows. And Siegfried is unconvinced. He tells her he sees only the billowing wave, and welcomes it even though it shatters his own image. He longs to merge with that stream and lose himself. He is supremely unattached to any sense of self.

This is the crux of the scene. Brünnhilde is wedded to her image of Brünnhilde just as much as she is to her image of Siegfried. She cannot see what she might be if she is not a Valkyrie. She longs for the place and role which her father took from her, and even though she cannot return to her past it makes her hesitate when Siegfried offers her the future. He is asking her to leap into the unknown, after all, inviting her to share in "that act whereby [they become] human through love,"[16] and this is terrifying because it does away with the ego she has been trying to hold on to and the world she has come to count on. Berger notes that "Wagner's comment on this kiss, noted in Cosima von Bülow's Diary (August 15, 1869), is significant and perceptive: 'The kiss of love is the first intimation of death, the cessation of individuality, that is why a person is so terrified by it.'"[17] But all bliss, for Wagner, depends on the acceptance of death.

Brünnhilde is right to see that love's rejoicing drives away heavenly wisdom. It drives away all wisdom of all sorts, all reliance on ideas and images. But she does really love the foolish boy, and as they embrace she sees at once what love grants them in recompense: it is the absolute trust which opens her to "radiant love / and laughing death." She and Siegfried both give themselves "wholly and entirely to reality—to encounter birth, growth, bloom, blight and decay frankly, with joy and with sorrow, and

---

16 *Letters to August Roeckel*, 83 (January 25–26, 1854), *SL* 303.
17 Berger, *Beyond Reason*, 136.

to live to the full this life made up of happiness and suffering—so to live and so to die."[18] Their final duet is a confession of love, of course, but genuine love, for Wagner, is always *amor fati*, the love of one's destiny, so at the same time they delight in all that may come, no matter the cost.

Even if the music were not so splendid Wagner would have had good reason to be proud of this work. It is drama and philosophical demonstration at one and the same time. His philosophy starts from the endless creativity of life and humanity's self-made separation from that movement. With that act we feel ourselves to be discrete individuals, torn between our longing for emotional fulfillment and the demands of social life. Yet that conflict exists only because we have blinded ourselves to what is real. Love, for Wagner, is what opens our eyes. It shows us that we are one with that activity which makes all things and all beings, its implicit order reflecting and responding to all that we and they do. The inner and the outer are as one.

This unification of the personal and the political lies at the heart of Wagner's utopian ideal, in which social life is made and remade through "the inexhaustible variety of the relations of living individualities to one another."[19] The very structure of *Siegfried* depicts the emergence of that dynamic unity, and it realizes his ambition of an artwork that brings home the complex identity of humanity and nature. Its love scene mirrors its fairy tale. Brünnhilde's inner transformation aligns her with the same surging necessity that explodes in the outer world. In both stories stasis and separation are swept away, and at the end of the drama we see Siegfried and Brünnhilde, together, the humanity of the future, embodying in their union "the actual, true and blissful common-being of *Mankind*."[20] In their leap from darkness to light, from fear to love, and from confinement to absolute spontaneity, they give us a momentary glimpse of a revolutionary dawn. But it is only a glimpse, only a moment. The ecstasy of the end of *Siegfried* will soon turn into the betrayals and brutality of the *Ring*'s tragic close.

---

18   *Letters to August Roeckel*, 59 (September 12, 1852), *SL* 270.
19   *Opera and Drama*, *PW* II, 203.
20   "Art and Climate," *PW* I, 261.

9: *Götterdämmerung*: The Deed that Redeems the World

THE STAGE SET for Act Two of *Götterdämmerung* shows the open entrance to the hall of the Gibichungs on the right and the banks of the Rhine on the left. A rocky hill rises diagonally from the shore, and paths lead up its slopes to a small altar for Fricka and larger ones for Donner and Wotan. These are sites for animal sacrifice, and in his scene with the vassals Hagen tells them to bring bulls for Wotan, a hog for Froh, a deer for Donner, and sheep for Fricka. The vassals comply; at the close of the act the processions of young men and women leading sacrificial beasts to flower-bedecked altars make an ironic backdrop for the personal dramas, Gutrune's and Siegfried's naïve happiness contrasted with Brünnhilde's and Gunther's suppressed fury.

Hagen knows, however, that the sacrifices he commands are pointless. In the dream colloquy that opens the act Alberich had told him that the gods will not answer. They have accepted their defeat and sit silently in Valhalla, paralyzed with fear and awaiting their end. The Wotan narrative is over. This was not the situation in *Siegfrieds Tod*, but all of Wagner's revisions to that text develop this theme, and he revised the staging of this act to heighten the dramatic irony of the useless rituals and the discord between the simple faith of the populace and the godless acts of their betters. In 1848 there had been no visible altars, and the sacrifices were offstage and made known only through the sounds of a "sacrificial song."[1]

The gods' silence is only part of a broader and deeper calamity. Wagner had a habit of presenting events and only later explaining them, as he does in the first act of *Die Walküre,* and the Norn scene with which he opens *Götterdämmerung* is another example of that procedure. It is here that we are told about Wotan and the fatal wound he inflicted on the world ash-tree. We learn, too, that the spring at its base, the source of the Norns' wisdom, had dried up. Like Erda in Act Three of *Siegfried*, they are unable to make sense of an increasingly clouded and confused future. At the end of their scene their rope snaps, worn thin by the effects of

---

1   Haymes, *Wagner's Ring in 1848*, 144–47.

Alberich's curse. They sink down to endless sleep with their mother Erda, lamenting the end to eternal wisdom.

Wotan had drunk from their wisdom-granting spring; it had cost him an eye. He had relied on what the spring revealed, both directly and through the Norns' nightly counsel, and we see now that one of the consequences of his own act was the end of this spring and its wisdom. The sense of the world is lost. Thanks to Wotan, it can no longer be read or communicated, to him or to anyone else.

The Norns' narration helps to explain Erda's confusion at her second appearance, and justifies Wotan's charge that she was no longer what she imagines herself to be. The wisdom of the primordial mother was coming to an end, he had told her, and this turned out to be the truth. But Wotan was wrong to tell her that this was because his own will now prevailed. He does will the end of the gods and his replacement by Siegfried, claiming to embrace the future with happiness and joy, but he had not grasped that the authority he was stepping away from had already faded. As Erda had told him, he was not what he called himself. Siegfried's easy triumph is perhaps due to the youth's reforging Nothung, but it may also be due to the twilight of Wotan's world-order, manifested in the finite life of his spear. The world ash-tree's slow dying is mirrored in the slow decline of his power, and Siegfried cuts through a spear that was already fatally weakened.

What the Norn scene brings home most powerfully is that this is now a world without transcendence. It is not yet a world with any other kind of cohesion, however; *Götterdämmerung* takes place in a kind of Gramscian interregnum, where the old world is dying and the new one is yet to be born. The human world in which the pursuit of the Ring now takes place is even less capable of dealing with its threat than Wotan's was, and that pursuit becomes nothing more than a conflict among individuals, worked out through plotting of the most superficial kind.

It is a critical commonplace that its origin in *Siegfrieds Tod* makes *Götterdämmerung* not a music drama but a heroic opera, replete with grand opera clichés like an oath scene, a conspiratorial trio that calls Meyerbeer to mind, a massed chorus, and so on. (Shaw saw this clearly.) There are implausible plot contrivances, too; the potion that causes Siegfried to forget Brünnhilde and fall passionately in love with Gutrune is the exception to the rule that Wagner's potions are symbols of inner transformation. This one is a potion which really is a potion. Siegfried raises the drinking horn, consecrates the first drink to Brünnhilde, and at his first sip loses all memory of her. This is so abrupt as to make psychological explanations dubious. They would be beside the point anyway.

Siegfried has very little inner life and no concealed or repressed motivations to be brought to the surface. He is already all on the surface.[2]

But so are most of the characters in this essentially melodramatic piece. "Siegfried is no more than a tool in Hagen's plot," wrote Dahlhaus, "playing hardly more independent a role than Gutrune and Gunther, who are saved from being boring only by their ambivalence." Even "Hagen and Brünnhilde ... are not much more than the vessels for certain unmitigated passions," and are not "characters in any true sense of the word."[3] This is the besetting sin of all melodrama, an essentially complacent form in which the dramatist elicits conventional emotional responses by displaying external collisions among static and easily grasped stereotypes.

In *Götterdämmerung* we scarcely notice this, so potent is the music. By this point in his career Wagner had an effortless control of dramatic action, and expressed it through continuous thematic variation and development, complex but lucid polyphony, a fluid harmonic language, and an orchestral pallette that has been a source of inspiration or outright theft for composers ever since. *Götterdämmerung's* "dramatic symphony" (this is Dahlhaus's term) gives life and depth to the often-superficial characters, ties the action to everything that has already taken place and to its all-encompassing mythological context, and enriches and comments on the events through its many preludes and orchestral interludes, Siegfried's Rhine journey and funeral music, of course, but also the two great sunrise interludes, after the first scene of the prologue and after the Hagen-Alberich scene, and much more.

For the most part the characters remain cardboard cut-outs, but there is a reason for this: they are two-dimensional people who live in a two-dimensional world. The human society of the Gibichungs is surely meant as an image of the nineteenth-century bourgeoisie—perhaps in Paris, which Wagner still dreamt of burning. It has removed itself completely from the necessity of the Real. Shallow and competitive, it revolves around externalities like prestige, displays of power, and the pursuit of luxury, as far as that was possible given the barbarism of the times. Gunther is the perfect image of Wagner's "Nature-sundered man," taking "his personal, egoistic, and therefore impotent being for the essence of the human species."[4] His first question of Hagen is about his reputation, and Hagen tells him that it is unfortunately low and that he would give it

---

2 Dahlhaus's interpretation is different but worth consideration: *Richard Wagner's Music Dramas*, 91.
3 Dahlhaus, *Richard Wagner's Music Dramas*, 134.
4 "Art and Climate," *PW* I, 260.

a boost if he could acquire a wife and get Gutrune a husband. This makes sense to Gunther, who is motivated by artificial needs alone. Rather than marry for love he wants to acquire a trophy wife, for display purposes, and for the same reason Gutrune must be married to a hero, the more famous the better. He is delighted with Hagen's scheme. They will drug Siegfried so he is besotted by Gutrune, have him seize Brünnhilde for Gunther by force, and celebrate a double wedding that will make the Gibichungs famous up and down the Rhine.

It is hard to interpret this superficiality as a product of Alberich's curse, but there does not need to be any causal connection. The Gibichung world is the perfect environment for the Ring, because the Ring embodies pure egoism, the result of Alberich's denial of love, and it consequently implies everything that motivates life in a social order built around the pursuit of personal power and fame. For self-enclosed, selfishly ambitious, and insecure men and women there could be no higher object of desire. Hagen will lure Gunther into full complicity with his murder plot by telling him he would have immense power if he took the Ring from Siegfried. Hagen would never let that happen, of course, but he knows just how tempting a suggestion this is.

Once Hagen uses the potion of forgetfulness to destroy his connection with Brünnhilde Siegfried fits into that order with disquieting ease. He had been the "man of the future," grounded in living reality through confident, egoless love, but with a sip of the drink he becomes just another man of the present, obsessed with externalities, eager to fit in, and with no mind to do anything but what everyone else would like him to do. Siegfried not only has no objections to Hagen's unspeakable scheme, he can barely wait to set it in motion. He and Gunther sail off without even taking a meal. Without Brünnhilde he is just another brutal male in a brutal world, incapable of compassion and deaf to the voices of women, and what he does to his beloved is rape in everything but the strict legal sense.

The potion did nothing but take away Siegfried's memory of Brünnhilde. It alone is not responsible for his brutality, which is, instead, the frightening converse of his essential lack of consciousness.[5] His violence is horrible enough standing alone, as it does in *Siegfrieds Tod*, but it is additionally terrible in the light of his history as Wagner developed it in the 1850s. Siegfried's mother had been forced to marry Hunding, and his father had made enemies of Hunding and his clan by trying to prevent another forced marriage. Siegfried repeats the pattern, but he puts himself

---

5   See Dahlhaus, *Richard Wagner's Music Dramas*, 90–91.

on the wrong side. At the end of Act One of *Götterdämmerung* he is forcing a woman he thinks he does not know to marry someone she has never seen. His act of violence betrays both his family and his bride and it makes him little different from the man who killed his father.

Siegfried has become his own antithesis, as Brünnhilde says in the Immolation scene: no oaths were sworn by anyone more honest, no contracts were made by anyone more true, and nobody else loved with more innocence; and yet nobody dishonored oaths, contracts, and love as he did. In *Siegfried* he was pure, selfless activity, so transparent and candid that she, too, could let go of all fixed ideas and surrender to the radiance of egoless love. For most of *Götterdämmerung* he is just the opposite. He has become the Hero with a capital H, not so much a human being but the impersonator of a social role that he has to burnish and uphold, and he sacrifices everything to that image.

This is clearest, perhaps, in the Act Three scene with the Rhinemaidens. Gorgeously written, this serves as a momentary relief from the gathering menace of the score, but it is also a turning point in the Alberich narrative; in it Siegfried seals his fate by choosing to hold on to the Ring. He enjoys the maidens' teasing, which is of the henpecked-husband variety, and for a moment, at least, he offers to toss them the Ring. They might have gotten it back, too, if they had not blundered into what Siegfried takes to be threats. They will not take it, they tell him, until he knows all about the curse; then he will be happy to be rid of it.

Siegfried, though, is famous as the person who knows no fear, and that image would not survive were he to be seen acting out of fear or even caution. Giving the Ring back after the Rhinemaidens' warning would look like an act of prudence, and this would be beneath his dignity. His mind is made up. Warned that he will die that day if he does not return the Ring, he throws his own life away; it means as little to him, he boasts, as the clump of sod he tosses over his shoulder. He writes his own death-warrant, not by his fearlessness but by his fear of being seen as fearful.

Wagner insisted that this was an act of "infinite wisdom":

> [Siegfried] has grasped the highest truth and knows that death is better than a life of fear: knowledge of the ring, too, has come to him, but he does not heed its power, for he has something better to do; he keeps it only as a proof that he at least has never learnt what fear means.[6]

---

6   *Letters to August Roeckel*, 103 (January 25–26, 1854), *SL* 309.

There is indeed something grand about Siegfried's gesture, but his wisdom seems very far from being infinite. Wagner was always prone to special pleading where Siegfried was concerned. His hero was never one for listening to wise counsel, and the Rhinemaidens are right that he is hobbled and blind; he has no idea of anything past the end of his nose, and keeping the Ring as a reminder of anything accomplishes nothing except the continuation of the curse. He certainly comes off poorly in his reflections on the conversation. He's learned how women are, he says; if they don't get their way with flattery they'll try threats. This is, at best, the wisdom of the frat house.

As Wagner had told Röckel, "Siegfried alone ... is not the complete human being: he is merely the half."[7] Brünnhilde, too, is not the complete human being once they are separated. Earlier in the drama she, too, had been given her own opportunity to return the Ring, and she, too, had refused. The Valkyrie Waltraute, distraught, had stolen away from Valhalla to tell her about the gods' fearful watch and Wotan's silence. Wotan still thinks of his favorite daughter, and he murmurs that the gods and the world would be free of Alberich's curse if she would only give the Ring back to the Rhinemaidens. That is what Waltraute has come to beg of her, and Brünnhilde says no. The Ring is Siegfried's love-token, she says, worth more to her than Valhalla's bliss and eternal glory; its light is the holy light of Siegfried's love. Waltraute, driven away, laments Brünnhilde's loveless obstinacy.

This seems like a selfish act, which it is, but Wagner sees Brünnhilde as motivated by love; she can do nothing else, since "from the moment that Siegfried had awakened her she has no other knowledge than the knowledge of love." The symbol of that love is the Ring, and he argues that, since only love is god-like, it is understandable that she will "let the splendour of Walhalla fall in ruins, [for] she will not give up the ring (her love)."[8] But this is only an explanation of her refusal, not a justification:

> [I]f you shudder because ... she should have preserved as a symbol of love just this ring on which the curse lay, then you will have penetrated my meaning, and will have understood the curse of the Nibelungs in its most terrible and tragic significance.[9]

Brünnhilde is right to value love above all else, but she has associated it with an object which is in every aspect malign. It is the wrong kind

---

7   *Letters to August Roeckel*, 98 (January 25–26, 1854), *SL* 307.
8   *Letters to August Roeckel*, 105 (January 25–26, 1854), *SL* 309.
9   *Letters to August Roeckel*, 106 (January 25–26, 1854), *SL* 309.

of object to be a symbol of love, and Brünnhilde's grasping it, like Siegfried's, makes the final calamity inevitable.

The nature of the object is not really of much importance, though. The problem lies deeper, disclosed and concealed by Wagner's identification of the Ring with Brünnhilde's love. These two are incommensurate. The Ring is just a piece of metal. It contains no love. What has passed and could pass between Siegfried and Brünnhilde is unaffected by any symbol, and the two will mean as much to each other whether or not Brünnhilde holds on to the Ring. In her isolation, though, Brünnhilde had bound herself to an object into which she has projected an image of past happiness, something finite and static, and finitude and stasis signal the death of love and, ultimately, death itself. The duet at the end of *Siegfried* had shown how difficult it had been for her to pull herself away from images and live in the ever-changing world of love, and when Siegfried leaves she falls back into old habits, doting on the memories and dreams she calls up when looking at the Ring as she had once been drawn to the memories evoked by her helmet and breastplate. She will not give it up even to heal the world.

Siegfried and Brünnhilde were, together, joyously open to "radiant love and laughing death." As they said farewell to each other Brünnhilde sang that even divided they would never part. They were indeed parted, though, and neither of them could maintain that blissful freedom. Both lost touch with what is fundamentally real, Siegfried betrays her, and she takes her revenge by plotting his death.

That death resolves nothing. It is as horrifying as Wagner meant it to be, and he stages it with unsurpassable pathos and grandeur. Siegfried is granted a moment of grace, as his memory returns to him and he imagines himself reunited with Brünnhilde, and when he dies the orchestra laments both his life and his wasted future in music that unites his story with that of the Volsungs in one granitic act of mourning. Yet Wagner knew, too, that Siegfried was not a tragic figure, "since he does not become conscious of his position, ... he is quite unaware, though the audience knows. Wotan and Brünnhilde are tragic figures."[10] He is just another victim of Alberich's curse, and his death carries no meaning and cannot bring the dramas to a close. That task is left for Brünnhilde. She must act to redeem the world.

Wagner was famously vague about what that act was and what it meant for the world to be redeemed. These had been reasonably clear in the first version of *Siegfrieds Tod*, even if the answers were trivial, but only a few months after he wrote that text he had replaced Siegfried's

---

10 Cosima Wagner, *Diaries*, vol. I, 653.

apotheosis with a new speech. Brünnhilde now placed Siegfried among the gods and then told them to "fade away in bliss before man's deed," proclaiming their "blessed redemption in death."[11] Things only got more complicated after that. In late 1852 Wagner had Brünnhilde impart her "most holy wisdom" to the world in the so-called "Feuerbach ending," which rejected everything but love; "love alone can be." This Beatles-like moral did not make it into the final score, and neither did the "Schopenhauer ending" of 1856, in which Brünnhilde announced that she had been redeemed from reincarnation and passed beyond desire and delusion, achieving "the blessed end of all things eternal."[12]

Wagner rejected these as "sententious." They were certainly that. The world was not going to be redeemed with a sermon. As drama, too, they could only have failed. The fifteen hours of the *Ring* had left Wotan walled up in Valhalla and Siegfried dead. The only free agent left was Brünnhilde, and as a protagonist she was called upon to do something both effective and necessary. She could not be passive, as Siegfried was, and whatever she did had to change the world, which is different from telling it how it should change. She could not walk away.

What, then, does she accomplish? Wagner despaired of giving answers to this question, finally rejecting all explicit messages in the hopeful belief that the music itself would be sufficient. It is still worth asking, even though any answer puts one on dangerous ground. It is helpful, first of all, to consider some of the things that she does *not* do. It is hard to accept the Jungian interpretations, which see Brünnhilde's fiery death as a symbol of personal transformation and the "sacred marriage" of animus and anima, not just for their fuzzy logic but because they leave few grounds for any emotional response. They could hardly justify the splendor of the music, and they are totally apolitical, too.

Richard Bell, in his voluminous recasting of the *Ring* as a Christian allegory, sees Brünnhilde as a Christ figure. She "seems to recover her divinity" in the immolation scene, he writes, and this event "is highly significant theologically."[13] But it is an event which does not occur. In *Siegfrieds Tod* she does regain her powers:

---

11 Stewart Spencer and Barry Millington, *Wagner's Ring of the Nibelung: A Companion* (New York: Thames & Hudson, 1993), 362. This anti-monarchical ending predates the Dresden uprising.

12 Spencer and Millington, *Wagner's Ring of the Nibelung*, 362–63 (both endings).

13 Bell, *The Theology of Wagner's Ring Cycle*, vol. I, 209; see also vol. II, 242.

> My Wisdom returns to me again,
> I recognize the ring's runes.
> I also understand the Norns' counsel,
> I can interpret their speech:
> The mightiest deed of the boldest man,
> My wisdom is able to bless it.[14]

This makes sense in terms of the earlier version of the ending: she would have to be immortal in order to pass through the pyre and bring Siegfried to Valhalla. But such a transformation is unnecessary at the end of *Götterdämmerung*, since Valhalla is about to burn down, and Brünnhilde would hardly choose to rejoin the gods just in time for their extinction. Those lines are omitted, and in their place Brünnhilde thanks the "wise sisters of the watery deep," the Rhinemaidens, for their sound counsel.[15] The point of Wagner's revision could not be more self-evident: his heroine dies as a mortal woman, not as a god.

More commonly held is the idea that Brünnhilde gives the spectators a powerful lesson in the importance of love. She does not do this by lecturing them, mercifully enough, but through action; when she puts the Ring on her finger and rides into the fire she and Siegfried are married once more, this time in the afterlife which is taken for granted throughout the cycle. It is hard to see this as a world-changing event, however, and as someone who had just helped in the murder of her husband it is not very persuasive. In *Götterdämmerung*, though not in the other dramas, love appears as something "quite thoroughly devastating."[16]

Others claim that Brünnhilde redeems the world by ending it. This is widely assumed to be what the end of the *Ring* is all about, but it is hard to defend. Wagner had his black moods, and leafing through his letters it is easy to find expressions of contempt for and condemnation of existence, but one has to set aside the text and music of the cycle itself to suppose that it depicts the last days of humanity. The stage directions speak twice of the men and women who watch those events, and nothing suggests that they are either incinerated or washed away, let alone that this is what they desire. Stewart Spencer supposes that "the end of the world is now a consummation devoutly to be wished" as "the bystanders accept that 'breaking of the will' which, according to Wagner, is the

---

14 Haymes, *Wagner's Ring in 1848*, 180–81.
15 *G* III, lines 2084–87.
16 *Letters to August Roeckel*, 151 (August 23, 1856), *SL*, 358, translation altered.

ethical theme of the Ring,"[17] but this is comically unsupported. There is also nothing of Schopenhauer about such a general massacre, either; the philosopher thought that suicide was a mistake, if an understandable one in certain instances, and he would never have countenanced mass murder. Over and above all that, it would be hard to honor or even tolerate Brünnhilde if she died with the blood of millions of humans and Nibelungs on her hands.

She clearly does not. Wagner is actually very specific about what happens at the end of the *Ring* and his stage directions give equally specific causes for those events, all of them naturalistic within its mythic presuppositions. The flames of the funeral pyre set the Gibichungs' hall alight and then die down, leaving a cloud of smoke. The Rhine overflows its banks and the Rhinemaidens swim in; they are water creatures and this is the only way they can retrieve the Ring. Once they have it, they and the flood waters return to the river bed. The clouds then part, and the spectators see Valhalla ablaze. Brünnhilde had sent Wotan's ravens to Loge, asking him to light the logs of the world ash-tree that surround the fortress, and he has followed her command. Nothing else is burning. There is no general destruction.

If Brünnhilde does not bring the world to an end, what does she do? The text of the Immolation scene offers at least one possible solution. Wagner has asked a lot of his spectators, and it was probably unrealistic for him to expect them to pay close attention to the words in a passage of such extraordinary musical eloquence, especially after hours of taxing events conveyed though music of exceptional immediacy and intensity. The words deserve close attention nonetheless; they contain no lessons to be learned, but they make Brünnhilde's intentions clear and show that her immolation is not merely an act of love for Siegfried. It is an offering on behalf of the world as a whole. Through the manner of her death she resolves the twofold crises of the Alberich narrative, both the Ring's absolute and arbitrary power and the curse that Alberich had laid upon it.

Brünnhilde reproaches the gods for their eternal guilt; they had doomed Siegfried to die by the curse that should fall on them, too, and he, the purest of men, had to betray her so she could become wise. That wisdom is complete; she says she knows "Alles, Alles, Alles"; everything is clear to her now. She wishes Wotan peace, in a famous passage of compassionate solemnity, and then says:

---

17 Spencer and Millington, *Wagner's Ring of the Nibelung*, 372.

> I now take my inheritance as my own,
> accursed Ring! frightful Ring!
> I take your gold
> and give it away. ...
> I give to you [the Rhinemaidens] what you covet;
> out of my ashes
> take it for your own.
> Let the fire that burns me
> cleanse the curse from the Ring
> let it dissolve
> in the flood.[18]

She takes the Ring, places it on her finger, and prepares to light the funeral pyre.

For the entire length of the cycle everyone, Wotan included, has acted as if everything would be resolved once someone gives back the Ring to the Rhinemaidens. Nobody does this, although Siegfried comes tantalizingly close, but if they had done so the titanic drama would have petered out in a deflationary anti-climax. What Brünnhilde understands is that this would still not have solved the problem. It reckons without the curse, which is something apart from the magic of the Ring itself. She speaks of these separately: "take it for your own," she says of the Ring, and then, in a new sentence, commands the fire to remove its curse. The Rhinemaidens get the Ring, and its curse dissolves to nothingness in the river: these are two independent events.[19]

Brünnhilde now knows how the curse must be undone. She knows, too, that this task is hers alone. Like Antigone, "[s]he knew, what she was doing,—but she also knew that do it she must."[20] The Ring's other victims, like Siegfried, had gone to their deaths without any awareness of the fatality that had caught them up. Brünnhilde, by contrast, acts deliberately. As broken as her life has become, it was still up to her to decide if she lived or died, and like Aida she chooses death, but in a way that makes herself into a sacrificial offering. She knows that it is not fire alone that removes the curse; if that were the case she could leave the Ring on Siegfried's finger. She knows, too, that there is only one way to put an end to it. She needs to embrace it. She needs to give herself up to it as its final victim.

---

18   *G* III, lines 2078–95, translation largely mine.
19   This may be implied by the parallel section of *Siegfrieds Tod* (Haymes, *Wagner's Ring in 1848*, 182–83), but it is far more pointed and explicit in the final version.
20   *Opera and Drama*, *PW* II, 189.

The fire that burns her body will burn away the curse, she says: in other words, Brünnhilde accepts the curse into herself so intimately and fully that one fire puts an end to them both. Her offering up of her death to lift Alberich's curse undoes a world-poisoning breach and redeems the world. It is an act of moral grandeur and tragic heroism, Wagner's highest form of dramatic action, where

> ... [the protagonist] proves the truth of his being not only in his own actions—which can, as long as he continues to act, still appear arbitrary—but by sacrificing his personality to the necessity of events. The last, most complete externalisation of his personal egoism, the presentation of his complete sublation into the universal is announced by his death, and no arbitrary death but rather a necessary one, one that is determined by his actions from the full force of his being.[21]

The first free character in the cycle, she dies to free all of humanity.

In the last section of the Immolation scene a theme appears that has been heard only once before, when Brünnhilde had told Sieglinde that she was bearing the world's greatest hero. What Sieglinde realized in that moment was that she had not lived and suffered in vain, and neither had Siegmund. Unless we are deaf to its lyricism, as Shaw was, we will hear it in the same way in the Immolation scene, and again, when it ends and resolves the tumultuous orchestral postlude: Brünnhilde's suffering and death, like Sieglinde's, will bear fruit and transform the world. The motif has been called "redemption through love" and Wagner called it "the glorification of Brünnhilde." Both names are appropriate; Brünnhilde, "offering [her] personal being itself in favour of the universal,"[22] redeems the world out of the same "pure Human love" that Wagner saw in Antigone, and through her "self-annihilation in the cause of sympathy" she, too, becomes "the perfect Human Being," a complete embodiment of the moral law. She deserves the benediction of the cycle's final bars. But the theme is also, as Borchmeyer calls it, "the motif of birth and

---

21 *The Artwork of the Future*, 79, *PW* I, 198–99. See also *Jesus of Nazareth*, *PW* VIII, 313: "the creature that fulfils this offering with consciousness, by attuning its free will to the necessity of this offering, becomes a co-creator,—in that it further devotes its free will to the greatest possible moral import of the sacrifice, however, it becomes God himself."

22 *Jesus of Nazareth*, *PW* VIII, 317.

rebirth," and Wagner noted that he completed the *Ring* on the birthday of his firstborn child, Isolde.[23]

The debates over the end of the *Ring* are endless—this small book will not put an end to them—but there is at least no need to choose between pessimism and optimism. Some things are obvious. The gods are not just silent, they are dead. Humanity is no longer threatened by the absolute and arbitrary power of the Ring, which could have forced people, individually or collectively, into slavery or some other fixed order, or by Alberich's curse. The local nobility are gone, too; the Gibichungs are dead and their hall is in ashes. Women and men are now liberated from every structure or source of power that had divorced them from natural necessity, and they are free to make of their world what they choose; as Wagner wrote in an early revolutionary essay, "since the Law is for the living, not the dead, and ye are living, with none conceivable above you, ye yourselves are the law, your own free will the sole and highest law."[24]

This is all to the good, but it does not lead to an optimistic or a pessimistic conclusion; we have no idea what they will make. It may be better than the world which has just come to an end, it may be worse—Alberich is still around—or it may be nothing but a reenactment of the same disastrous errors. The curtain falls, though, on a world with no gods and no masters. *Götterdämmerung* ends in a radical openness to the future.

---

23 Dieter Borchmeyer, *Drama and the World of Richard Wagner*, trans. Ellis (Princeton, NJ: Princeton University Press, 2003), 236.
24 "The Revolution," *PW* VIII, 236.

10: Epilogue: After Transcendence

The *Ring* cycle takes between fourteen and fifteen hours to perform. Its length is its most obvious feature, something which seems to be both unnecessary to point out and unimportant to consider. As Tovey said, however, the scale of a work is by no means irrelevant: "Macaulay once shrewdly observed that the size of the Great Pyramid was essential to its sublimity, 'for what could be more vile than a pyramid thirty feet high?'"[1] The same is true of the *Ring*. Its sublimity is inseparable from its length and from the necessity of performing it over four successive days (or over a week, with days off in between each part). Attending a complete cycle usually requires something like a pilgrimage, which is exactly what Wagner intended, and its parallel and intersecting narratives, its all-enveloping musical texture, and its constant linking of present moments to past moments contribute to the sense we often have that we are inhabiting the work rather than merely watching it. Characters and events are with us when we arise the morning after a performance and live with us until we rejoin them in the afternoon. The *Ring* becomes an experience, a period in one's life on which one can look back and contemplate.

The cycle is structured and coherent as life is not, but just as "life lessons" trivialize real life, the *Ring* is trivialized when it is reduced to morals or to lessons of varying banality about the values one should adopt. It is not hard to pick out plot points and dialogue to support the idea that it is about the superiority of love over power, but that opposition must be set among others—separation and self-surrender, individualism and community, finitude and infinitude, stasis and transformation, concept and reality—and all these must be understood as existing only provisionally, as artifacts of our self-separation within a world which is profoundly one. Whether or not we attain that understanding, in turn, defines two different worlds and the shapes of human life which are appropriate and possible within them. One world is composed of self-seeking (but actually self-denying) individuals, their lives regulated and coordinated by external

---

1 Donald Francis Tovey, *Essays in Musical Analysis*, vol. II (Oxford: Oxford University Press, 1935), 4. Tovey was, as usual, quoting from memory, and I have not found the original Macaulay text.

structures—humanity "kept only on the straight and narrow by property or laws," at risk of sliding into chaos if there is no ordering power. In the other a liberated humanity continually forms and reforms itself, its actions grounded in openness, mutuality, and flexibility, a moral world-order shaped by "the inexhaustible variety of the relations of living individualities to one another."[2] Only in the second world is genuine love possible. In the first it is just egoism à deux, no more than a respite from the stress and sterility of the everyday.

The *Ring*'s tragic heroes, Wotan and Brünnhilde, are both caught between those two worlds, between the hidden but all-powerful movement of the real and their drive to shape, control, or avoid that activity, and both identify themselves with ideas of their own making, unaware that this removes them "farther than ever from the reality of the world."[3] Brünnhilde, like the rest of humankind, cannot bear very much of that reality. She repeatedly seeks to define herself or take refuge in images. She hesitates to leave behind her identity as a Valkyrie, although she does so at the end of *Siegfried,* and when she is once more left alone on her rock she retreats into an unproductive, even dangerous egoism. She wants to stop time and deny change, fixing her memories of Siegfried's love and projecting them into an object so she can relive them at will. Her struggles suggest how hard it can be to rise above ideas of the self.

Wotan does much the same thing in the political realm, making a fetish of the world-order that he had shaped. His response to the threat of the Ring shows how the preservation of a legal or political structure can

---

[2] A digression: Wagner's opposition has a much broader philosophical context. It maps well onto the implicit political implications of Leibniz-Clarke correspondence, for example. The Newtonian cosmos is composed of discrete and fundamentally static entities which are maintained in order only by the laws of a creator god, while Leibniz suggests a relational, self-organizing cosmos in which all is in motion and everything depends on everything else. As Steven Shapin has famously shown, Clarke saw Leibniz's physics as a threat to the principles of order on which the Glorious Revolution rested ("Of Gods and Kings: Natural Philosophy and Politics in the Leibniz-Clarke Disputes," *Isis* 72, no. 2 [1981]: 187–215). Such ideas were doubly disturbing to Clarke because they suggested the implicit panpsychism and pantheism of Anthony Collins and John Toland, two other targets of his attacks, and likely because similar ideas had been associated with such Civil War radicals as Gerrard Winstanley. This was not so much a "Radical Enlightenment" as it was an alternative ontology, reflected in Kant's physics and an unacknowledged influence on Diderot and also Fichte; as I hope to show in a forthcoming essay, the *Wissenschaftslehre* can be read as a demonstration that the Newtonian cosmos is simply the phenomenal form of the relational, Leibnizian one.

[3] Paraphrasing *Letters to August Roeckel*, 81 (January 25–26, 1854), *SL* 302.

become an end in itself. Confronted with Alberich's ambitions he will do "whatever it takes" to defend his world and protect the law against lawless outsiders. That defense, though, becomes more important than anything else, including the maintenance of justice and humanity within the law-bound community, and the belief that these two can be kept apart is a delusion. Wotan finds himself compelled to sacrifice his own children to the War on Alberich.

Throughout the *Ring* Wagner explores the price we pay for trying to force reality into the mold of our concepts, and part of its fascination is how he sees this at work in the personal, political, and ethical realms. He grasps how intertwined these are, and never reduces one aspect to any other. This may be an additional reason that the *Ring* seems to show us a living world. But it shows us, too, that the problems of that world cannot be resolved by adopting a new and improved set of basic ideas. Its crises have not come about because Wotan relied on mistaken concepts. It fails because relying on concepts can do nothing but wall us off from life itself.

Experience is finite by necessity. As Fichte wrote at the outset of his career, the human mind "is enclosed within a circle that it itself has drawn around itself."[4] Nobody escapes this problem. The differences among human worlds lie in the particular limits they draw and in the ways through which they acknowledge or fail to acknowledge that this is what they have done.[5]

The present day does not come off that well in that respect. It is as limited as every other possible world, but it is especially flawed in that it is built on a denial of that fact. It claims to encompass everything. This mirrors what Wittgenstein wrote in connection with science:

> 6.371 The whole modern conception of the world is founded on the illusion that the so-called laws of nature are the explanations of natural phenomena.
>
> 6.372 Thus people today stop at the laws of nature, treating them as something inviolable, just as God and Fate were treated in past ages. And in fact both are right and both wrong: though the view of the ancients is clearer in so far as they have a clear and acknowledged

---

4 Johann Gottlieb Fichte, Zürich lectures, February 26, 1794, in Fichte, *Foundations of the Entire "Wissenschaftslehre" and Related Writings*, trans. Breazeale (Oxford: Oxford University Press, 2021), 448.

5 It can be reasonably argued that most religious traditions, with the signal exception of Christianity, function to critique or deconstruct the necessary illusions of self-consciousness.

terminus, while the modern system tries to make it look as if everything were explained.[6]

We think we live in a fully transparent, rational world, but that belief comes from the fact that our limits are not imposed from the outside but lie within, in our embrace of the inherent illusions of self-awareness, and so we cannot see them.

Our present world-order is contract-based, like Wotan's, and is inhabited by people who cannot imagine themselves to be anything but individuals, called upon to make lives shaped by nothing but their own interests and beliefs. Such a world-order asks very little, only "an erroneous view of the essence of the Individual," a separation of the personal from the social. That separation, though

> ... is a rupture in our hearts, a split which runs through each of us and cuts us off from our corporeal selves. We no longer acknowledge the thought of the body, through which all of us together generate and recreate our selves and our worlds. Identifying ourselves with our conscious existence alone, we are driven further and further within, seeking a "true" nature unsullied by the demands of the world. ... And as we identify ourselves with the shrinking and increasingly barren territory within which we can pretend to exercise true autonomy, the same separation between individual and social worlds leaves us powerless to change anything in the sphere of the social. We are free but impotent.[7]

This split is closely akin to what Wagner saw at the dawn of self-consciousness, and he had Jesus teach that this impotence comes about through the malignant growth of the state and individuals' despairing retreat into infantile egoism. The resulting sterility has a fitting image in the death of the tree of life and of the spring and its wisdom.

This has serious consequences for everyday politics, too. If we are nothing more than individuals the public sphere must fade away, replaced by a playing field on which we all compete, and the only allowable freedom becomes Isaiah Berlin's negative liberty. Common action appears to be a delusion, no more than ideological cover for private interests. A consistent individualism leaves no room for the broader and deeper life of

---

6   Ludwig Wittgenstein, *Tractatus Logico-Philosophicus*, trans. Ogden (London: Kegan Paul, Trench, Trübner & Co., 1922), 181.

7   Michael Steinberg, *The Fiction of a Thinkable World: Body, Meaning, and the Culture of Capitalism* (New York: Monthly Review Press, 2005), 163–64 (including quote in previous paragraph).

reality, and thus our common life, the source and foundation of ethics, remains hidden and is not even thinkable. Morality becomes privatized. We can strive to live decent and ethical lives, but we must live them within what is, at best, an amoral society which has been emptied out of content to make room for individuals' private choices. This sounds liberating until we realize that our world can never be fundamentally different from the way it is now.

That is why, as Wagner insisted, no new world could be made with the laws of the present. But where could we find any others? Any world grounded on mutuality has to begin with something beyond the bare fact of mutuality; we need some common principles if we are to talk meaningfully with each other, plan out our actions, and resolve our disagreements. Those principles are not self-evident. We might think that they could be found within, in our deepest longings for a better life, but that "within" is just another product of the imagined separation of self and world, and when we think we have found our way to pristine human nature what we discover is only an internalized reflection of the "outside." There is no social change that is not a change in personal life, and no change in personal life is possible without social change. That, however, just makes the problem harder, and both Wagner and Fichte knew this.

Nietzsche called for a new mythology, decades after Hegel and his roommates had done the same, but mythologies do not drop down from the heavens, as the "Earliest Program" had foretold,[8] and without the kind of collective, communistic creativity that Wagner extolled the new mythology would inevitably end up as another form of top-down control. In his *System of Ethics* Fichte insisted that a genuine community could shape itself through the incessant redefinition of a *Symbol*, which he said had no explicit content beyond the assertion that the supersensual was real. The German word *Symbol* has two meanings, however; it can mean "symbol" but it can also mean "creed," and it was hard for Fichte to untangle this concept from that of a common church to which everyone must belong.[9] It was a short road from there to the exclusion of Jews from the community, and Muslims, too, if anyone had thought of them back then. Something similar is, of course, found in Wagner, overtly in his antisemitism and obliquely elsewhere.

Fichte also tried to ground community in language, arguing in the *Addresses to the German Nation* that German, uniquely among European languages, maintained its connection with the life of an organic

---

8   "Earliest Program for a System of German Idealism," 73.
9   Fichte, *System of Ethics*, 224.

community.[10] Only in German could the supersensual speak. This was implausible and lent itself to a racist nationalism in spite of Fichte's overt intentions; he himself thought that non-Germans could learn the language and assimilate themselves to the life of the German-speaking *Volk*. Such two-faced toleration was hardly welcoming to others, though, and Wagner would never go even that far; he insisted that while Jews could learn and speak German, they would inevitably do so as foreigners.

Wagner's ambitions for Bayreuth suggest another possibility, the creation of a community through art, and this idea was to have many consequences through the late nineteenth and early twentieth centuries—most if not all of them bad. "Wagnerism" and the "religion of Bayreuth" were both failures, and they were so from the beginning. When he first came up with the idea of the *Ring* Wagner wanted admission to be free.[11] The expense of staging such a massive work forced him to surrender this fantasy, and instead of the first festival being an assembly of the people it was attended by the wealthy and titled, with at least three kings in the audience. The dream was a forlorn one anyway. The *Gesamtkunstwerk*, Wagner had argued, could never be "the wilfully possible act of a single mind but ... [was] the necessarily conceivable collective work of humankind of the future."[12]

He tried to create such a work nonetheless, and what he achieved remains thought-provoking and valuable even today; the unstoppable stream of new interpretations is testimony to that. This book is not meant to refute or replace any of those, but it does highlight one aspect of Wagner's accomplishment. The *Ring* is, among many other things, a deep and broad critique of the world in which Wagner lived. It is equally a critique of our own.

A critique, however, only closes off dead ends. We are still left without a guide. Any alternative future way of life remains unknowable, opaque. Even its starting point is hidden. We may decide, like Karol Berger, that the only grown-up course of action is to accept that we live in a broken and delusion-ridden world and make the best of our fallen state, since, as Mrs. Thatcher said, there is no alternative. If there really is no alternative, though, then we must also consent to driving ourselves into a world ever more perilous to us and to our non-human brethren, ever more impoverished in terms of biological diversity, and ever more

---

10 The interconnections between this and his proposed national education were never clearly developed.
11 This was his ideal for all drama; see *Art and Revolution*, PW I, 63–64.
12 *The Artwork of the Future*, 23, PW I, 88.

devoid of spontaneous human interaction or even common civility. The *Ring* shows us that world, and the complexity and occasional grandiosity of Wagner's vision makes us feel that we have been shown the fate of every imaginable scheme to manage it and every dream of transforming it from within. These are one and all undermined by the primal delusion of self-consciousness, the belief in our separation from the other, whether it be nature or our fellow humans, which is not a fact at all but only the necessary precondition of self-awareness, something which we fail to recognize and so cannot see or feel our way beyond. James Treadwell has argued that the *Ring* keeps being pulled back towards its origins and to Alberich's curse.[13] His point is well taken, but what he notices is not a defect. We are confined within the circle we have drawn for ourselves, and Wagner has dramatized our world's inability to step outside of it; but he has also suggested in its closing bars that our hope for a different world need not be delusional.

For all of Wagner's emotional nastiness and intellectual indiscipline, he understood the poison at the root of his and our world and how it courses through our veins and feeds all its injustices and miseries, in the cultural sphere and in economic and social life. He understood the longing to build an unpoisoned community which did not drive humanity apart from nature and humanity from itself. He felt these issues viscerally, and he was able to body them forth in poetry, dramatic action, visual imagery, and above all in music, all put in the service of essentially philosophical insights. Through its long gestation the *Ring* became much more than an unreasonably long opera. Wagner created a work which stands alone, a mythic tragedy understood through some of the fundamental insights of the early idealists and the Jena Romantics, ideas which remain among the most radical in the history of European thought. These are found, too, in the "Earliest Program for a System of German Idealism," which lay unknown and unpublished until 1917. Wagner could not have been aware of that manifesto, but his concerns, insights, and hopes were close to those of its authors, and the *Ring* carries out some of their project. It makes mythology philosophical and makes philosophy sensuous and mythological, in the hopes of bridging the educated and uneducated so they might bring about a world of "universal freedom and equality." It is a great work of art, but it is also the most unexpected monument of classical German philosophy.

---

13 Treadwell, *Interpreting Wagner*, 88–91 and elsewhere.

Appendix: A Note on Schopenhauer

Wagner had finished the poem of the *Ring* by the end of 1852. He first read Schopenhauer almost two years later, in October, 1854, when he was working on the composition of *Die Walküre*, and *The World as Will and Representation* was, he told Liszt, "like a gift from heaven."[1] He wrote to Röckel that Schopenhauer's philosophy "completely demolishes the nonsense and charlatanism of the Fichte-Schelling-Hegel view,"[2] and that it repudiated what he now thought of as the "heartless unreasoning optimism" of Judaism.[3] The philosopher had somehow known what he himself had intuited but not recognized, that the *Ring* was a demonstration of the nothingness of all existence, and Schopenhauer's ideas had led him to "the only adequate key-stone to my poem in keeping with the whole idea of the drama, which consists in a simple and sincere recognition of the true relations of things and complete abstinence from the attempt to preach any particular doctrine."[4] Yet he left the text of the dramas and their all-important stage directions unchanged. With respect to the *Ring* Schopenhauer offered little, it seems, but an after-the-fact interpretation, making Wagner the first of the many commentators on his work.

The suddenness of this conversion calls for an explanation. Wagner's own thinking had looked back to the philosophy of the first quarter of the century, and he may well have felt an affinity for Schopenhauer because Schopenhauer was, in reality, firmly in the tradition of early German idealism. The philosopher's persistent polemics against "the Fichte-Schelling-Hegel view," as Günter Zöller says, "appear more as deliberate attempts to distance himself from competing approaches and to more starkly highlight his own philosophical contributions than might have been warranted by the fact of the matter."[5] He had studied with Fichte in 1811–1812, and the first edition of *The World as Will and Representation* appeared in

1   Letter to Franz Liszt, December 16, 1854, *SL* 323.
2   *Letters to August Roeckel*, 123 (date uncertain).
3   *Letters to August Roeckel*, 139 (date uncertain).
4   *Letters to August Roeckel*, 150–51 (August 23, 1856), *SL* 358.
5   Günter Zöller, "Schopenhauer's Fairy Tale about Fichte: The Origin of *The World as Will and Representation* in German Idealism," in *A Companion to Schopenhauer*, ed. Bart Vandenabeele (Oxford: Blackwell, 2012), 387.

1817. Zöller's essay shows just how indebted it was to Fichte's late philosophy and just how far Schopenhauer went to conceal that influence.

That effort was and is surprisingly successful. Michael Tanner writes that "Schopenhauer is the first philosopher to make our contact with the world primarily a matter of will, rather than perception or reason," and that this was "no doubt the ultimate reason why [Wagner] found Schopenhauer so congenial and liberating."[6] As a matter of history this is simply wrong; Fichte had argued decades before Schopenhauer that neither perception nor discursive reason offered any direct contact with reality, which could be apprehended only through action and the emotional states that arose from each act. A similar insight was clearly present in Wagner's texts from 1848 through 1851; if he did not arrive at it on his own he certainly did not get it from Schopenhauer.

He surely responded to Schopenhauer's pessimism, which explained and justified his own frequent black moods, but the philosopher's arguments about the centrality of will, "the subjective character of all phenomena," and "the difference between intellectual conceptions and intuitions"[7] were hardly original and likely impressed Wagner because they, too, were consistent with ideas he had picked up and developed himself.

Wagner's "conversion," though, unfortunately put an end to his own philosophical development. Instead of working through his own insights he deferred to Schopenhauer, reading his works again and again and referring to him as if he were an all-wise authority. Yet he was an inconsistent and often heterodox Schopenhauerian. In 1858 he wrote to Mathilde Wesendonck to tell her that he had discovered "the path to salvation, which has not been recognized by any philosopher, and especially not by Sch[openhauer], but which involves a total pacification of the will through love, and not just through any abstract human love, but a love engendered on the basis of sexual love." He planned to explain this to the philosopher and add that artistic genius was "an intensification of the individual intellect to the point where it becomes an organ of perception of the genus or species, and thus of the will itself, which is the thing in itself; herein lies the only possible explanation for that marvellous and enthusiastic joy and ecstasy felt by any genius at the highest moments of perception."[8]

---

6 Michael Tanner, *Wagner* (Princeton, NJ: Princeton University Press, 1996), 206.

7 *Letters to August Roeckel*, 128 (date uncertain), 152 (August 23, 1856), *SL* 358.

8 To Mathilde Wesendonck, December 1, 1858, *SL* 432. In the end he did not write to Schopenhauer.

Such a "correction" would be nothing less than a repudiation of one of Schopenhauer's foundational ideas, that the Will which engenders all phenomena is essentially blind and destructive, so that "salvation" is freedom from its impulsions, not identification with them. There is no place for "marvellous and enthusiastic joy and ecstasy" in Schopenhauer's world, either.

Wagner's "corrections" sound like a simplified version of his own ideas from the early 1850s, and they are also reminiscent of Fichte's "blessed life," which is egoless participation in the one life of the divine. They account for the grandeur that attends his portrayal of Tristan and Isolde, whose fatal passion suggests a deeper and more blissful truth than could ever exist in the light of the everyday, and for our response to that drama, which is very far from the dispassionate pity that would be the most that Schopenhauer could muster. Those ideas inform much of the *Ring*, as well. Neither the love between Siegmund and Sieglinde nor that between Siegfried and Brünnhilde ends well, but neither of them is presented as delusional or as a product of the trickery of the Will. There is no sense of irony or distancing in their scenes together. Those are uncomplicatedly affirmative, moments of light which make the surrounding shadows all the darker, and they could not serve this function if we saw them as Schopenhauer would.

Wagner took what he wanted from Schopenhauer and ignored or creatively misunderstood the rest, and when he attempted to insert his version of his idol's ideas into his dramas he usually failed. The "only adequate key-stone" to the *Ring* that he mentioned to Röckel was the 1856 "Schopenhauer ending," but this presents such a jarring contrast with the rest of cycle that it would have given audiences whiplash injuries. Brünnhilde was to sing that she would close behind her "the open gates of eternal becoming" and attain "the goal of the world's migration"; she, the enlightened woman, would be "redeemed from reincarnation."[9] Wagner could almost have been versifying a recent essay on Schopenhauer: "When this final enlightenment is achieved, then man understands that the dream of life can be awakened from; it is then that the pain of tragedy is replaced by the benign indifference of salvation from both the world and the self."[10] The Immolation scene, however, does not depict "benign

---

9   Spencer and Millington, *Wagner's Ring of the Nibelung*, 369.
10 David Becker, "Schopenhauer on the Meaning of Tragedy: Vision and Blindness," *Schopenhauer Jahrbuch 91* (Würzburg: Verlag Königshausen & Neumann, 2010), 30.

indifference," and Brünnhilde would cut an unsympathetic figure indeed if that was how she left the world.

As drama, too, this speech would fail. Not one of those ideas had played any part in the fifteen hours of action or dialogue that reach their culmination in this scene. The most egregious interloper is the notion of reincarnation, which is completely inconsistent with the afterlife as it had been presented in *Die Walküre* and undermines the Immolation scene itself. Brünnhilde was well aware of what happens after death, given her job as a Valkyrie; in the *Ring* universe some kind of personal existence continues, either in Valhalla or in Hella.[11] The "Schopenhauer ending" replaces this with reincarnation and a quasi-Buddhist release from the cycle of death and rebirth. Wagner could not make that substitution, though, without doing violence to his own text.

On top of that, the enlightenment that Brünnhilde claims would make nonsense of the ecstatic greeting to Siegfried in her final lines. Tanner dismisses these as the ravings of a woman "in an advanced state of delusion. She will not be embraced by Siegfried, because he is dead, and there will be no Valhalla for them to go to, since in a moment it will be going up in flames."[12] But in the world presented in the *Ring* death is not the end, and the destruction of Valhalla does not require the abolition of the afterlife. It is perfectly sensible for Brünnhilde to imagine that she and Siegfried will be reunited in Hella, just like the Volsung twins. Her final words are not delusional, then, unless she does indeed find release from reincarnation, for that alone would rule out any posthumous embrace.

The Schopenhauer ending is thus not just insufferably self-righteous; it pulls the rug out from under the rest of the drama and makes its heroine into a fool who looks forward to both personal extinction and a lovers' reunion at the same time. Wagner was right to remove it, and later interpretations of the cycle in the light of Schopenhauer's ideas have usually led to equally questionable results.

These often construe Wotan's weariness as a desire for the end of everything, even in his *Die Walküre* monologue, which ignores the scene in *Siegfried* when he tells Erda he would leave his lordship to Siegfried, and they see the end of *Götterdämmerung* as a picture of the end of the world. Wagner did sometimes say this, but I myself find that interpretation hard to square with the music. That is a subjective argument, of course, but it is consistent with the more objective argument that was set

---

11 Hella is simply the afterlife in Norse mythology, and it should not be confused with the Christian Hell.

12 Tanner, *Wagner*, 178.

out in chapter nine: it is contrary to the text. It also descends into fantasy by assuming some mysterious causation that converts a pair of localized fires into a full-fledged *Weltuntergang*.

These events are not elements in some apocalypse. They resolve specific lines of narrative in specific ways. This is what successful drama does, and Wagner was nothing if not a consummate theatrical craftsperson. His metier, however, set him at odds with the philosopher whom he idolized. Schopenhauer's philosophy left no room for meaningful human action or for dramas with any real content. He read Greek tragedy as a demonstration of the meaninglessness of life, a showing of the inherent horror of being a tool and a victim of a destructive impersonal Will, and this devalues the specific events of any given tragedy. In his view they all taught the same lesson: it is best of all never to have been born.[13]

This cannot be what the *Ring* is all about. Its interweaving narratives, its all-but-inexhaustible richness and variety, its fully realized major and minor figures, the sense we have that we have come face to face with fundamental human realities, and its sophisticated treatment of social and political issues and the interplay between inherent and contingent factors in the maintenance of social and political order—all this and more would disappear if its only message was the nothingness of existence or the worthlessness of the world, a hell beyond saving which is fit only for Alberich.[14] That could not be even *one* of its messages, because it would swallow up everything else like a black hole. Schopenhauer is no guide to Wagner's intentions in the *Ring*. These are clear from the work itself, which ends not in deathly silence or compassionate resignation but in the hope that the human community can be made anew or, at the minimum, in the confidence that human life can be worth its inevitable tragedies.[15] As Dahlhaus says, "Brünnhilde's love for Siegfried … looks forward in hope to reconciliation in the future," to "the freedom of the human consciousness," and "[t]he music Wagner wrote in 1874 to bring *Götterdämmerung* to its conclusion expresses just that."[16]

---

13 Becker, "Schopenhauer on the Meaning of Tragedy," 21.
14 So says Warren Darcy, taking one of Wagner's bleaker outbursts for a reasoned conclusion, in "'The World belongs to Alberich!' Wagner's changing attitude towards the 'Ring,'" in Spencer and Millington, *Wagner's Ring of the Nibelung*, 52.
15 Williams, *On Opera*, 86.
16 Dahlhaus, *Richard Wagner's Music Dramas*, 141.

Works Cited

By Wagner

The Artwork of the Future. Trans. Emma Warner. London: The Wagner Journal, 2013.
Letters to August Roeckel. Trans. Eleanor C. Sellar. Bristol: J. W. Arrowsmith, 1897.
My Life. "Authorized translation." New York: Dodd, Mead & Co., 1911.
Richard Wagner's Prose Works. Trans. William Ashton Ellis. 8 volumes. Lincoln and London: University of Nebraska Press, 1993–1995. Abbreviated as *PW*.
The Ring of the Nibelung. Trans. John Deathridge. London: Penguin Classics, 2018.
The Ring of the Nibelung. Trans. Stewart Spencer. In Stewart Spencer and Barry Millington, *Wagner's Ring of the Nibelung: A Companion.* New York: Thames & Hudson, 1993.
Selected Letters of Richard Wagner. Trans. and ed. Stewart Spencer and Barry Millington. London: J. M. Dent, 1987. Abbreviated as *SL*.
"Siegfried's Death" and "The Nibelungen Myth." In Edward Haymes, *Wagner's Ring in 1848.* Rochester, NY: Camden House, 2010.

Other Authors

Arkle, Robyn. "Gustav Mahler and the Crisis of Jewish Masculinity." *19th-Century Music* 47, no. 3 (2024): 157–75.
Auden, W. H. *The Dyer's Hand and Other Essays.* London: Faber and Faber, 1948.
Authorship disputed. "Earliest Program for a System of German Idealism." In *Theory as Practice: A Critical Anthology of Early German Romantic Writings*, ed. Jochen Schulte-Sasse et al. Minneapolis: University of Minnesota Press, 1997.
Becker, David. "Schopenhauer on the Meaning of Tragedy: Vision and Blindness." *Schopenhauer Jahrbuch 91.* Würzburg: Verlag Königshausen & Neumann, 2010.
Bell, Richard. *The Theology of Wagner's Ring Cycle*, 2 volumes. Eugene, OR: Cascade Books, 2020.
Berger, Karol. *Beyond Reason: Wagner contra Nietzsche.* Berkeley: University of California Press, 2017.

Berry, Mark. *Treacherous Bonds and Laughing Fire: Politics and Religion in Wagner's "Ring."* London and New York: Routledge, 2006.
Berry, Mark, and Nicholas Vazsonyi, eds. *The Cambridge Companion to Wagner's "Der Ring des Nibelungen."* Cambridge: Cambridge University Press, 2020.
Borchmeyer, Dieter. *Drama and the World of Richard Wagner.* Trans. Daphne Ellis. Princeton, NJ: Princeton University Press, 2003.
———. *Richard Wagner: Theory and Theatre.* Trans. Stewart Spencer. Oxford: Clarendon Press, 1991.
———. "Wagner and Nietzsche." Trans. John Deathridge. In *The Wagner Handbook*, ed. Ulich Müller and Peter Wapniewski. Cambridge, MA: Harvard University Press, 1992.
Callow, Simon. *Being Wagner.* New York, Vintage Books, 2017.
Clark, Christopher. *Revolutionary Spring: Europe Aflame and the Fight for a New World, 1848–1849.* New York: Crown, 2023.
Cooke, Deryck. *An Introduction to Wagner's "Der Ring des Nibelungen."* Decca Records insert, n.d.
———. *I Saw the World End.* Oxford: Oxford University Press, 1979.
Coren, Daniel. "The Texts of Wagner's *Der junge Siegfried* and *Siegfried.*" *19th-Century Music* 6, no. 1 (1982): 17–30.
Corse, Sandra. *Wagner and the New Consciousness: Language and Love in the Ring.* Rutherford, NJ: Fairleigh Dickinson Press, 1990.
Craft, Robert. *Stravinsky: Chronicle of a Friendship.* Nashville, TN: Vanderbilt University Press, 1996.
Cutler, Robert M. "Bakunin's Anti-Jacobinism: 'Secret Societies' For Self-Emancipating Collectivist Social Revolution." *Anarchist Studies* 22, no. 2 (2014): 17–27.
Dahlhaus, Carl. *Wagner's Music Dramas.* Trans. Mary Whittall. Cambridge: Cambridge University Press, 1979.
Darcy, Warren. *Das Rheingold.* Oxford: Clarendon Press, 1993.
Deathridge, John. *Wagner Beyond Good and Evil.* Berkeley: University of California Press, 2008.
Deathridge, John, and Carl Dahlhaus. *The New Grove Wagner.* London: Macmillan, 1984.
Donington, Robert. *Wagner's Ring and its Symbols.* London: Faber & Faber, 1969.
Evans, Richard. *The Third Reich in Power, 1933–1939.* New York: Penguin Books, 2005.
Feuerbach, Ludwig. *The Essence of Christianity.* Trans. George Eliot. New York: Harper & Row, 1957.
———. *Thoughts on Death and Immortality.* Trans. James A. Massey. Berkeley: University of California Press, 1980.
Fichte, Johann Gottlieb. *Addresses to the German Nation.* Trans. George A. Kelly. New York: Harper & Row, 1968.
———. *The Characteristics of the Present Age.* In *The Popular Works of Johann Gottlieb Fichte.* Trans. William Smith. London: John Chapman, 1859.

———. *Early Philosophical Writings*. Ed. and trans. Daniel Breazeale. Ithaca, NY: Cornell University Press, 1988.
———. *J. G. Fichte and the Atheism Dispute (1798–1800)*. Trans. Curtis Bowman. Farnham and Burlington, VT: Ashgate, 2010.
———. *The System of Ethics According to the Principles of the Wissenschaftslehre*. Trans. and ed. Daniel Breazeale and Günter Zöller. Cambridge: Cambridge University Press, 2005.
———. *The Vocation of Man*. In *The Popular Works of Johann Gottlieb Fichte*. Trans. William Smith. London: Trübner & Co. [4th ed.] 1889.
———. *The Way to the Blessed Life*. In *The Popular Works of Johann Gottlieb Fichte*. Trans. William Smith. London: John Chapman, 1859.
———. Zürich lectures, February 26, 1794. In Fichte, *Foundations of the Entire Wissenschaftslehre and Related Writings*, trans. Daniel Breazeale. Oxford: Oxford University Press, 2021.
Frank, Manfred. *The Philosophical Foundations of Early German Romanticism*. Trans. Elizabeth Millán. Albany: SUNY Press, 2003.
Garrett, Clarke. *Respectable Folly: Millenarians and the French Revolution in France and England*. Baltimore: Johns Hopkins University Press, 1975.
Hegel, G. W. F. *The Difference Between Fichte's and Schelling's System of Philosophy*. Trans. H. S. Harris and Walter Cerf. Albany: SUNY Press, 1977.
———. *Elements of the Philosophy of Right*. Trans. H. B. Nisbet. Cambridge: Cambridge University Press, 1991.
———. *Faith and Knowledge*. Trans. Walter Cerf and H. S. Harris. Albany: SUNY Press, 1977.
———. *Hegel's Logic, being Part One of the Encyclopedia of the Philosophical Sciences*. Trans. William Wallace. 1873; reprint, Oxford: Clarendon Press, 1973.
———. *The Phenomenology of Spirit*. Trans. A. V. Miller. Oxford: Oxford University Press, 1977.
Heine, Heinrich. "Am I a Destroyer of Faith?" In *The Poetry and Prose of Heinrich Heine*, trans. David Ewen. New York: Citadel Press, 1948.
Henrich, Dieter. "Fichte's Original Insight." In *Contemporary German Philosophy, Volume 1*. Ed. Darrel E. Christensen, et al. Trans. David R. Lachterman. University Park: Pennsylvania State University Press, 1982.
———. "The French Revolution and German Philosophy." In Henrich, *Aesthetic Judgment and the Moral Image of the World: Studies in Kant*. Trans. Wayne Martin and Sven Bernecker. Stanford, CA: Stanford University Press, 1992.
Kant, Immanuel. *Critique of Pure Reason*. Trans. Norman Kemp-Smith. London: Macmillan & Sons, 1933.
Kierkegaard, Søren. *The Sickness Unto Death*. Trans. Alastair Hannay. London: Penguin, 1989.
Kitcher, Philip and Schacht, Richard. *Finding an Ending: Reflections on Wagner's Ring*. Oxford: Oxford University Press, 2004.
Magee, Brian. *Aspects of Wagner*. 2nd ed. Oxford: Oxford University Press, 1988.

———. *Wagner and Philosophy.* London: Penguin, 2001.
Mann, Thomas. "Sufferings and Greatness of Richard Wagner" and "Richard Wagner and the Ring." In Mann, *Essays of Three Decades*, trans. H. T. Lowe-Porter. New York: Knopf, 1948.
Marx, Karl. "Letter to Arnold Ruge of September, 1843." In Marx, *Early Writings*, trans. Rodney Livingstone and Gregor Benton. New York: Vintage Books, 1975.
———. "Theses on Feuerbach." Trans. unknown. https://www.marxists.org/archive/marx/works/1845/theses/index.html.
Matenko, Percy, Edwin Zeydel, and Berte Masche, eds. *Letters to and from Ludwig Tieck and His Circle: Unpublished Letters from the Period of German Romanticism Including the Unpublished Correspondence of Sophie and Ludwig Tieck.* Chapel Hill: University of North Carolina Press, 1967.
Mathäs, Alexander. "Self-Perfection—Narcissism—Paranoia: Ludwig Tieck's 'Der blonde Eckbert.'" *Colloquia Germanica* 34, no. 3/4 (2001): 237–55.
Millington, Barry. "Myths and Legends." In *The Wagner Compendium*, ed. Millington. London: Thames & Hudson, 1992.
Nattiez, Jean-Jacques. *Wagner Androgyne.* Trans. Stewart Spencer. Princeton, NJ: Princeton University Press, 1993.
Neumann, Peter. *Jena 1800: The Republic of Free Spirits.* Trans. Shelley Frisch. New York: Farrar, Straus and Giroux, 2022.
Nietzsche, Friedrich. "The Birth of Tragedy" and "Ecce Homo." In *Basic Writings of Nietzsche*, trans. Walter Kaufmann. New York: Modern Library, 1968.
Novalis. *Philosophical Writings.* Trans. Margaret Mahoney Stoljar. Albany: SUNY Press, 1997.
Reinhardt, Hartmut. "Wagner and Schopenhauer." Trans. John Deathridge. In *The Wagner Handbook*, ed. Ulich Müller and Peter Wapniewski. Cambridge, MA: Harvard University Press, 1992.
Rezneck, Samuel. "The Social and Political Theory of Mikhail Bakunin." *The American Political Science Review* 21, no. 2 (1927): 270–96.
Sansone, David. "Wagner, Droysen and the Greek Satyr-Play." *Antike und Abendland* 61, no. 1 (2015): 1–9.
Rilke, Rainer Maria. *Rilke on Love and Other Difficulties.* Trans. John J. L. Mood. New York: Norton, 1975.
Schlegel, Friedrich. "Dialogue on Poesy." In *Theory as Practice: A Critical Anthology of Early German Romantic Writings*, ed. Jochen Schulte-Sasse et al. Minneapolis: University of Minnesota Press, 1997.
———. *System of Transcendental Idealism.* Trans. Peter Heath. Charlottesville: University of Virginia Press, 1978.
Shapin, Steven. "Of Gods and Kings: Natural Philosophy and Politics in the Leibniz-Clarke Disputes." *Isis* 72, no. 2 (1981): 187–215.
Shaw, George Bernard. *The Perfect Wagnerite.* New York: Dover, 1967.

Spencer, Stewart, and Barry Millington. *Wagner's Ring of the Nibelung: A Companion*. New York: Thames & Hudson, 1993.

Steinberg, Michael. *Enlightenment Interrupted: The Lost Moment of German Idealism and the Reactionary Present*. London and New York: Zero Books, 2014.

———. *The Fiction of a Thinkable World: Body, Meaning, and the Culture of Capitalism*. New York: Monthly Review Press, 2005.

———. "How to Change the World: Cultural Critique and the Historical Sublime in the Addresses to the German Nation." In *Fichte's Addresses to the German Nation Reconsidered*, ed. Daniel Breazeale and Tom Rockmore. Albany, SUNY Press, 2016.

Steiner, George. *Antigones*. New Haven, CT: Yale University Press, 1996.

Tanner, Michael. *Faber Pocket Guide to Wagner*. London: Faber and Faber, 2010.

———. *Wagner*. Princeton, NJ: Princeton University Press, 1996.

Thompson, E. P. *Whigs and Hunters: The Origin of the Black Act*. New York: Pantheon, 1975.

———. "Work-Disciple and Industrial Capitalism." *Past & Present* 38 (1967): 56–97.

Tovey, Donald Francis. *Essays in Musical Analysis*. Oxford: Oxford University Press, 1935.

Treadwell, James. *Interpreting Wagner*. New Haven, CT: Yale University Press, 2003.

Wagner, Cosima. *Diaries*. Trans. Geoffrey Skelton. New York: Harcourt Brace Jovanovich: 1978.

Williams, Bernard. *On Opera*. New Haven, CT: Yale University Press, 2006.

Wittgenstein, Ludwig. *Tractatus Logico-Philosophicus*. Trans. C. K. Ogden. London: Kegan Paul, Trench, Trübner & Co., 1922.

Zenkovsky, V. V. *A History of Russian Philosophy*. Trans. George L. Kline. New York: Columbia University Press, 1953.

Zöller, Günter. "Romanticism as Modernism: Richard Wagner's 'Artwork of the Future.'" In *The Palgrave Handbook of German Romantic Philosophy*, ed. E. Millán Brusslan. London: Palgrave Macmillan, 2020.

———. "Schopenhauer's Fairy Tale about Fichte: The Origin of *The World as Will and Representation* in German Idealism." In *A Companion to Schopenhauer*, ed. Bart Vandenabeele. Oxford: Blackwell, 2012.

Index

Aeschylus 91
Alberich
   appearance of 100
   character of 42
   curse of 109–112, 114–115, 118, 120–121, 129
   in Nibelung myth 65–70
   renunciation of love 73–74, 112
Antigone 51, 95–96, 119–120
antisemitism x, 42–43, 101–102, 128
art, philosophy of 34–39
Auden, W.H. 1

Bakunin, Mikhail
   explains failure of revolution 50
   friendship with Wagner and Röckel 47
   imprisonment 49
   influenced by Fichte xi
   religion 48
Bell, Richard x, 116
Berger, Karol 41–42, 103, 107, 128
Berry, Mark 2
Borchmeyer, Dieter 12, 44, 91, 120
Breker, Arno 43
Brünnhilde
   actions for love 93
   acts to redeem the world 115–116
   choice to be destroyed by love 106–108
   compared to Antigone 95, 119–120
   defiance of father 94
   early character of 67
   egoism and love 124
   fathering of 89
   glorification of 120
   immolation scene 118–120, 133–134
   love of Siegfried 106
   refuses to give up Ring 114–115
   saves Sieglinde 93
   waking of 103, 105

Callow, Simon 47
Chéreau, Patrice 42
Clark, Christopher 48
Clough, Arthur Hugh 47
contractual order 75–77
Cooke, Deryck 33, 62, 68, 75, 93–94, 102
Coren, Daniel 62–63
Cornelius, Peter 1
Corse, Sandra 2
Counter-Reformation 11

Dahlhaus, Carl 59, 75, 87, 111, 135
Darcy, Warren 61–62, 81–82
Deathridge, John 60
Donington, Robert 6, 73

Erda
   conception of Brünnhilde 89
   endless sleep 110
   as oracle 82–83, 89–90, 93, 105
   speaking as the voice of nature 80–81

Fafner
   asks for Ring 83
   holds Ring 90, 102
   kills Fasolt 81
   murder of 66, 103–104
   as worker type 78
Fasolt 78, 81, 102
Feuerbach, Ludwig
   Essence of Christianity 23, 30
   influences Wagner x, 21

Principles of the Philosophy of the Future 24
Thoughts on Death and Immortality 22–24, 27, 50
Wagner's first encounter with 27–28
Fichte, Johann Gottlieb
  Addresses to the German Nation 54–56, 127–128
  Characteristics of the Present Age 54
  divine life 18–19, 133
  gives interpretive distance xii
  human agency 17, 125
  idealism 24
  influences Wagner xi, 41–42, 51
  Kant's philosophy 12
  life as collaborative activity 9, 14–15, 17–18, 31
  moment of insight 6–7, 14
  one life 28
  popularity of 12–13
  productive period x–xi
  and Schopenhauer 131–132
  System of Ethics 16, 127
  view of the self 15
  Vocation of Humanity 15–16
Freia 64, 102

Geist 37
Gibichungs 68, 94, 109, 111–112, 118, 121
Greek culture 42, 67, 82, 95, 135
Gunther 111–112
Gutrune 110–112

Hagen 65, 68, 90, 98, 109, 111–112
Hegel, Georg Wilhelm Friedrich
  absolute idealism 19–21
  on Antigone 51
  criticism of Fichte 19
  "Earliest Program for a System of German Idealism" 18, 47, 127, 129
  influences Wagner xi
  Phenomenology of Mind 20
  Philosophy of History 27

Hegelians, Left 3, 21
Hegelians, Right 21
Heine, Heinrich 21
Hella 134
Henrich, Dieter 17
Hitler, Adolf 43
Hölderlin, Friedrich 47

idealism, absolute. *see* Hegel, Georg Wilhelm Friedrich
idealism, German 3, 24, 29, 31, 131
idealism, transcendental 13–14

Jena Romantics 17, 129
Jews 42–43, 101–102, 127–128
Judaism 131

Kant, Immanuel 3, 8, 12–14, 96
Kitcher, Philip ix, 75

Loge 77–78, 84–85, 89, 118
Ludwig II of Bavaria 99

Magee, Brian ix, 5
Mann, Thomas 1–2, 60, 72
Marx, Karl 24–25, 56, 94
Mime 78, 100–105
Mythos 35–36, 38, 60

National Assembly 43–44
Nattiez, Jean-Jacques 4, 36
Nazism 43, 101
Nibelungs
  enslavement 64–65, 78
  freeing of 66–67, 74
  hoard of 64–65
  mythos of 60
  as proletariat 77
Nietzsche, Friedrich 3, 32, 127
Norns 65, 69, 80, 109–110, 117
Nothung 62–63, 110
Novalis 17–18

Ragnarök 65
Reformation 11
Rhinemaidens 72–73, 81, 85, 113–114, 117–119

Rilke, Rainer Maria   xii
Ring
   as absolute power   83–85
   in 1848 drafts   64–67
   as pure egoism   112
   relationship to Wotan's spear   69
Röckel, August
   friendship with Bakunin   47–48
   imprisonment   49
   Die Volksblätter   44
Romanticism   13, 17–18, 25, 35, 94, 129
Rosenzweig, Franz   13
Ruge, Arnold   56

Schacht, Richard   ix, 75
Schelling, Friedrich Wilhelm   18, 27, 34–35, 47, 131
Schlegel, Friedrich   18
Schopenhauer, Arthur
   influence on Wagner   28, 64, 118, 131–135
   "Schopenhauer ending"   116
   on suicide   118
   Wagner's reaction to   x, xii–xiii
   and Wotan   103
Semper, Gottfried   48–49
sexuality   22, 24, 32–34, 132
Sharon, Yuval   7
Shaw, George Bernard   5–6, 64, 77–78
Siegfried
   birth of   102
   brutality   112
   change in character   113
   death of   115
   early character of   100, 103–104
   forgets Brünnhilde   110
   as Hero   104, 113
Sieglinde   87–88
Siegmund   87–89
Sophocles   xi, 51, 91, 95
spear of Wotan   61, 62–63, 68–69, 75–76, 106, 110
Spencer, Stewart   117

Tanner, Michael   2, 132, 134
Thompson, E.P.   78, 83

Tieck, Ludwig   xi, 13, 17, 31
Tovey, Donald Francis   123
Treadwell, James   46, 129

uprising of May 3, 1849   48

Valhalla
   as afterlife   67, 77, 89, 93, 134
   building of   7, 64, 66, 74, 82, 85, 89
   burns   81, 117, 118, 134
   as haven for gods   80, 84, 89, 109, 114, 116–117
   as power   84
Valkyries   61, 67, 77, 88–89, 97
Vazsonyi, Nicholas   3
Verdi, Giuseppe   5

Wagner, Adolf   xi, 12–13, 31
Wagner, Richard
   antisemitism   42–43
   Art and Revolution
      art as revolutionary   38, 42, 49
      and Wagner's philosophy   3
   art as a form of revelation   34–39, 59
   Artwork of the Future
      art as human nature   21, 34, 45–46
      and consciousness   4
      on individuality   53–55
      on orchestra and voice   71
      on property   52
      and Wagner's philosophy   3
      writing of, in Switzerland   x, 49
   birth of   12
   common principles   127
   Communication to My Friends   3
   Götterdämmerung
      Brünnhilde and the Ring   114–121
      Brünnhilde's final words   117
      conclusion   60
      contemporary parallels   79, 111
      "Feuerbach ending"   116
      final scenes   118
      opening of Act I   109
      opening of Act II   109

relationship to *Siegfrieds
Tod* 64, 67–68
"Schopenhauer ending" 116,
133–134
Siegfried and the
potion 110–113
Siegfried and the
Rhinemaidens 113–114
on individualism 51–56
Jesus of Nazareth
and egoism 53–54
significance of love 51–53
and Wagner's philosophy 3
writing of 50
Der Junge Siegfried
composition of text 60
dragon in 104
foundation of *Siegfried* 59
Wotan's spear in 62–63
letters to August Röckel
on a better world 50
on Brünnhilde's love 96
on creation of art 6
end of the gods 84
on life and death 31–32
on reality 28
on Schopenhauer 131
"Schopenhauer ending" 133
Siegfried as half human
being 114
on Siegfried's
consciousness 104
significance of love 51
Wagner's philosophy 3, 4
Wotan the Wanderer 56
on Wotan's pride 105–106
Wotan's spear 63–64
and Ludwig Feuerbach 22–23,
27–28
"Man and Established
Society" 44–45
Die Meistersinger 99
*Nibelung Myth as Draft for a
Drama* 60–65
Opera and Drama
analysis of Sophocles 51–52
concept of love 96
historical argument 30, 92–93

mythic material 91, 95–96
on orchestra 72
and Wagner's philosophy 3
writing of 49
philosophy of creation and
destruction 28–29
response to
Schopenhauer 131–135
as revolutionary thinker 43–49
Das Rheingold
Alberich's theft 73–74
composition of text 60
early plot 61–62
Erda 80–82
gods in 64
opening 72, 74
reflects contemporary social
structures 78–80
relationship to Nibelung
myth 98
Wotan's rule 74–77, 83–85
self-awareness 29–31
on sexual love 22, 32–33
Siegfried
as fairy tale 102–103
as height of Ring cycle 100
Mime and Siegfried 103–105
relationship to *Der Junge
Siegfried* 104
Siegfried and
Brünnhilde 106–108
as Wagner's greatest
work 99–100
Wotan's return 105–106
Siegfrieds Tod
Brünnhilde regains her
powers 116–117
composition of text 60
foundation of
Götterdämmerung 59
invention of 44
plot 66–67, 104
relationship to
Götterdämmerung 64
social egalitarianism 41–42
on Sophocles 51–52
Tristan und Isolde 23, 88, 99,
105, 133

Die Walküre
    Brünnhilde's defiance   93–94, 96–97
    composition of text   60
    early plot   61
    opening of   87–88
    order versus creativity   92–93
    relationship to Nibelung myth   61
    spear of Wotan   63–64
    Valkyries stir up violence   89–90
    Wotan's farewell   98
    Wotan's monologue   90–92
Wesendonck, Mathilde   132
Williams, Bernard   79
Wittgenstein, Ludwig   125–126
world ash-tree   69–70, 109–110, 118

Wotan
    character of   74–75, 89
    destroys world ash-tree   109
    drinks from wisdom-granting spring   110
    early character of   67–68
    egoism and world order   124–125
    entrance in *Das Rheingold*   80
    love for Brünnhilde   97–98
    monologue   90–92
    relationship to Alberich   68–70
    return as king of the gods   105
    spear of *see* spear of Wotan
    as wanderer   103

Zöller, Günter   2–3, 9, 13, 131–132

www.ingramcontent.com/pod-product-compliance
Lightning Source LLC
Chambersburg PA
CBHW070808230426
43665CB00017B/2530